The Game Changer (Vol. 3)

Inspirational Stories that Changed Lives

Compiled by Iman Aghay

with

Denise Thomas, Darlene Coquerel, Connie Queen,
Christine Bennet-Clark, Kerry Cadambi, Kyra Lober,
Kimberly Hobscheid, Kathleen Carlson, Dale Schroeder,
Kat Halushka, Justin James, Jackie Simmons, Pamela Allen,
Melodee Meyer, Mayadari del Sol, Matilda Jarmy,
Marilyn Sutherland, Stephanie Duffey,
Shauna Marie MacDonald, Laura Cornell

The Game Changer (Volume 3): Inspirational Stories That Changed Lives

©2018 by Success Road Enterprises. All rights reserved.
Print Book ISBN: 978-0-9980350-0-0
eBook ISBN: 978-0-9980350-1-7

Published by Success Road Enterprises | Spotlight Publishing™

No part of this publication may be reproduced, distributed, or transmitted in any form or by any means, including photocopying, recording, or other electronic or mechanical methods, without the prior written permission of the publisher, except in the case of brief quotations embodied in critical reviews and certain other non-commercial uses permitted by copyright law.

Cover Design: Angie Analya
Interior Design: fiverr.com/aalishaa

Ordering information: Copies of this book may be ordered directly from www.mylifechangingmoment.com

The Game Changer (Vol. 3)

Inspirational Stories that Changed Lives

Compiled by Iman Aghay

with

Denise Thomas, Darlene Coquerel, Connie Queen,
Christine Bennet-Clark, Kerry Cadambi, Kyra Lober,
Kimberly Hobscheid, Kathleen Carlson, Dale Schroeder,
Kat Halushka, Justin James, Jackie Simmons, Pamela Allen,
Melodee Meyer, Mayadari del Sol, Matilda Jarmy,
Marilyn Sutherland, Stephanie Duffey,
Shauna Marie MacDonald, Laura Cornell

The Game Changer

Introduction

I've been working with entrepreneurs and other successful professionals for the past sixteen years. As a business mentor, I see the complex interworking of an entrepreneur's life. I have the privilege of knowing what goes on behind the scenes. I am humbled when I see what it takes for entrepreneurs to realize their achievements.

The Game Changer Book Series is a collection of these behind-the-scene stories — stories that most people never realize have laid the foundation for a successful business or company. These stories are personal, connected to the authors' hearts, and many of them are being shared for the first time with you, our reader. As I read this collection, I could not stop thinking about this old adage: *"Everyone you meet is fighting a battle you know nothing about! Be kind, always…."*

This book reveals some of the hardest times and darkest moments that entrepreneurs live through. Their experiences are real and deeply personal. Many of the chapters tell of bad choices and overcoming mistakes. However, all of them share something in common: a turning point — the turning point that changed the author's life forever. These stories are very dear to each author, and I am honored to be able to share their experiences with you. I hope that each of these stories touches you as deeply as I have been touched.

-Iman Aghay

The Game Changer

Table of Contents

Introduction *by Iman Aghay* v

Chapter 1: Poor as Church Mice *By Denise Thomas* 1

Chapter 2: Let Go and Let God *By Darlene Coquerel* 15

Chapter 3: No Mistakes *By Connie Queen* 27

Chapter 4: Being Who I'm Becoming
By Christine Bennet-Clark 37

Chapter 5: Wisdom Resides in the Body
By Kerry Cadambi 49

Chapter 6: A Wise Woman's Journey
By Kyra Rosalind Lober 61

Chapter 7: The In-Between Summer
By Kimberly Hobscheid 73

Chapter 8: Pretending No More
By Kathleen Carlson 85

Chapter 9: The Testing of Your Faith
By Dale Schroeder 97

Chapter 10: From Solitude to Sisterhood
By Kat Halushka 111

Chapter 11: From Invisible Leader to International Speaker *By Justin James*............ 121

Chapter 12: Looking into the Eyes of my Father *By Jackie Simmons*............ 131

Chapter 13: Another Level *By Pamela Allen*............ 143

Chapter 14: Author of My Life *By Melodee Meyer*............ 155

Chapter 15: Turning Points are Disguised Blessings *By Mayadari del Sol*............ 167

Chapter 16: It's About Time — and Intuition *By Matilda Jarmy* 185

Chapter 17: "All In" *By Marilyn Sutherland*............ 195

Chapter 18: You Can Only Save Yourself: A Lesson in Resiliency *By Stephanie Duffey*............ 211

Chapter 19: His Voice – His Limp – His Smile *by Shauna Marie MacDonald*............ 223

Chapter 20: #MeToo - How I Healed from Incest to Awaken to the Divine Feminine Within *By Laura J Cornell, PhD*...... 233

Chapter 1

Poor as Church Mice

By Denise Thomas

"You're too smart to be a pencil pusher all your life. Go get a degree." My dad worked for the Federal Reserve Bank at the time and the suggestion had come from his manager, so Dad took it quite seriously. As an Army veteran, Dad was able to pay for night school with the G.I. Bill. For many years, I watched as Mom stayed awake late into the night, helping him study for his exams. Then I sat in wonderment as he walked across the Tulane University stage to receive his diploma. I was only 10 years old.

In the 1970s, going to college wasn't as common as it is today. More kids would say they were "going into the family business." But for as long as I can remember, my parents never said, "IF you go to college." It was always, "WHEN you go to college." It was just assumed that college was our destiny. Dad knew what it was like to be a "pencil pusher"; he wanted a better life for his four kids, of which I am the oldest.

Growing up, we always had a roof over our heads, food on the table, and clothes on our backs. I had no idea we were poor as church mice. I thought Dad was handy because he would cruise the neighborhood the night before trash day, to see if there was any good junk he could refurbish...a desk, a rocking chair, a bicycle. "Take a ride with me," he would say. "Let's see if we can find some good junk." What a fun game! None of us realized our bikes were hand-me-downs from each other. As one would outgrow a bicycle, Dad would repaint it, slap on a new seat and streamers and, voila! Christmas! My mother never bought anything unless it was on sale.

Ever!! That's probably why I have a really hard time spending money on myself today. My grandmother, a seamstress, would make my clothes from other people's quilts and clothing. She would hold up a piece of newspaper, draw a few marks on it, and cut out a pattern. That was all so cool. I didn't realize it was by necessity.

In my teen years, I earned my spending money by babysitting and teaching other kids how to play the guitar. At age 16, I also started working for a large department store. I never really saved a penny of my earnings, and I always ate fast food for work lunches. As for high school, I was a good student, but not great. I was taking honors classes and had just over a 3.0 GPA. Then the summer between my junior and senior year of high school, I learned something that rocked my perfect little world. The topic of paying for college came up, and lo and behold, my mother said, "Oh, no. We're not paying for you to go to college. That's all on you."

Imagine my shock and disbelief! With this sudden revelation, the math flashed before my eyes. All those Taco Bell and Burger King lunches and dinners during my work day added up to a semester of college. I immediately started bringing a sack lunch instead. But, what about my 3.0 GPA? A 3.0 should get me a scholarship! Or so I thought. The universities recalculated my GPA without the honors credits, so my GPA became a 2.996... missed it by 'that much'. (Let's just say that my next sibling, a year behind me, didn't take honors classes that next year! Live and learn.) After doing some digging, it turned out that I was eligible for a federal grant to cover my college tuition, but I still needed to cover room, board, and textbooks.

Despite working several part-time jobs during my time at the university (at the cafeteria, the library, as a resident assistant, and eventually in the math department), I was barely scraping by. My bank held my tuition check for a few days until payday, so it wouldn't bounce. I remember sneaking cups of milk and fried chicken out of the cafeteria on Fridays so that I would have food for the weekend. (This was before Ramen noodles were invented!) I never thought of this as a hardship; I just felt privileged to be able to go to college. Figuring out how to squirrel away enough food for the weekend was a challenge…a game even. Then, once a year, my parents would visit, and Dad would slip a $20 bill in my hand when he said his goodbyes. (That was a lot of money for me, and for him.) He would say, "Get something decent to eat. Get some pasta!"

On school breaks, I worked that same retail job I had in high school, putting in as much overtime as possible. I was re-hired every summer and management would ask, "I see the last time you were here, you were paid $x per hour. How's that sound?"

I would casually mention that tuition had increased, and they would give me a raise. I think they were always so generous because they knew that they could count on me to work overtime and to work in any area of the store they needed.

During the summer between my last two years in college, I married my college sweetheart. Three months after our wedding, my mom passed away very unexpectedly. In helping my family sort through her things, I realized she had almost nothing. My mom literally owned only one bra, but she always made sure that her kids had almost everything. Now, as a parent, I understand that my kids always come first.

By the time I received my own diploma, I had taken out a student loan for my last year of school. My new husband also had school loans. By today's standards it wasn't a lot of money, but I still remember being eight years after graduation and weighing the cost of a .99 cent magazine at the grocery store checkout.

Fast forward ten years...I had just decided to homeschool the first of my two children for kindergarten. My husband and I had no definite educational plans for them, just that we would homeschool until either it wasn't working, or it wasn't fun anymore. I figured if we decided to stop homeschooling, 'they'- the school system-would have to take them back, since it's the law! Besides, when parents homeschool, they don't have to get up at 6 a.m. to put their children on a school bus!

Over the next few years, we moved several times due to my husband's work, homeschooling all the way. When my son was a year old, we were thrilled to move back to our home state, Louisiana. Not long afterward, my mother-in-law pointedly brought up how good the private schools were in the area. My reply, "Yes. ma'am. It costs $2000 per year. You payin'?" I never heard another word about putting our kids in "real" school after that.

Just three years after moving back to Louisiana, we built our dream home, a two-story home on a lake, with an open floor-plan and a downstairs big enough to hold church events. It was a blessing to be able to open our home to the youth and women's groups. It was everything we wanted it to be.

I continued to homeschool our kids. When our oldest, Brandi, was 12 years old, she asked if we could homeschool for high school. I had not thought that far in advance. We were still doing this one year, one textbook, at a time. So, when she said, 'high school', my brain went straight from high school, to college, to "Oh, crap! Was that even legal? Was I capable? Would she even be able to get into college as a homeschooled student?" Suddenly, I became aware of both the academic and financial responsibility we were facing. I had roughly a year to figure out the academic side and only a few more to figure out the financial.

Then, just a few months after moving into our dream home, my husband was laid off from the company for which he had worked nearly fifteen years. And what followed proved to be what felt like "a comedy of errors."

After a few months had gone by, my husband was hired by an engineering contracting firm, and we could breathe again. But we knew we couldn't afford to keep our dream home. We found a smaller home in a rural town for a great price, so we bought it before putting our dream home on the market. This was Error #1. Our timing couldn't have been worse. A month after buying house number two, the Twin Towers fell on September 11, 2001. We were at "war", and the economy was in recession.

We kept our dream house on the market, but barely had any action for months on end. When we finally found a buyer, they insisted on buying the house on a "bond for deed," which is a bit like buying a car because the seller still owns the home and the buyers pay monthly installments toward a purchase-to-own. This would prove to be Error #2.

The buyers of our beautiful home quickly began complaining about things we had no control over, like the electricity going out during a storm. They stopped paying the note on the house but didn't move out. That's when we learned that, legally, they could stay in the house as long as six months without paying before we could evict them. We were back to the sad reality of having two house notes again. To make matters worse, when the stock market tanked in the latter part of 2002, my husband was laid off yet again.

We removed what little money we had left in the failing stock market to cover two house notes and living expenses. Eating out was limited to Taco Bell's dollar menu with a free cup of water. We did what we could for as long as we could. In the end there was only enough left to buy a trailer and a lawnmower and start a lawn care business. But we were already out of time.

We had no choice but to declare bankruptcy and sell everything, absolutely everything, for mere pennies. I had accumulated a home school library of over 500 books. Some had yet to be opened. Everything in the kitchen, the furniture, the toys…nothing was untouched. Having a garage sale is one thing. Having strangers invade my home and make an offer on the pot I was cooking our dinner in is a whole different feeling. We even had to let go of our two dogs. I was absolutely devastated, and my heart still aches for them. Yep, we were poor as church mice.

Both houses went into foreclosure, and we moved into a tiny apartment 40 miles away. We were able to find a complex that allowed us to keep the trailer, so my husband could start the lawn care business. In less than a year, we were able to grow the company from nothing to five figures. Within two years we no longer had to advertise for business. It ran strictly on word of mouth. However, since we couldn't get health insurance for me, we hired my brother-in-law to help with the business, so my husband could get a job offshore for the insurance benefits. He worked two weeks at a time and was home to run the lawn business the other two weeks per month. We were making it work.

We moved two more times before Brandi would start home-schooling high school. We moved into a rental home but discovered we needed a residence that could accommodate the large trucks that were becoming imperative to our growing business. So, we moved into another rental, a boathouse on a river. We loved the location and the view, and the price was right. A year later, just as we started Brandi's ninth grade year, Hurricane Katrina hit. It was more than six weeks before electricity would be returned to the area. Upon returning, we discovered that the boathouse had shifted during the storm, necessitating another move.

Because Brandi was officially in high school, I knew I had to get serious about college finances. She was a good student and had unique extracurricular activities and leadership roles, but would that be enough? Just like my parents before me, I knew my husband and I couldn't afford to pay for her college. Moreover, I didn't want my children to struggle for every penny the way I had. Co-signing for a loan would be out of the question, and I didn't want student loans for either of my children.

I began researching colleges, with input from Brandi. Being a mom, I thought an all-girls school would be a great idea! She didn't go for that. Her main criteria was that it had to be south of the Mason-Dixon line. For those unfamiliar with the term, it meant she wanted to stay in the southern United States. She is a southern girl, and she doesn't do "cold" weather. We initially toured seven colleges, both public and private, across three states. As we were driving to my alma mater, she began to cry. When I asked what was wrong, she said, "I'm afraid I'm going to love it. And I know we can't afford it." That broke my heart. I said, "If this is where God wants you to go, He'll make it happen." In my head I was praying, "God, don't make me a liar!" And of course, like her mother, she absolutely fell in love with that school.

From then on, I spent almost every night until the early morning hours researching colleges and scholarships, making spreadsheets, trying to figure out how to manage college finances. I looked into having her join organizations that gave scholarships to their members, but being homeschooled, most would not grant her membership. Many of the larger scholarships began with pages of checklists of typical high school sponsored activities to weed out the tens of thousands of applications they got each year. However, almost none of those activities were available to homeschooled students. It seemed the deck was stacked against us.

When she was a junior, we had our first break. It had been a shot in the dark. She had started a business when she was 16 years old, and this national scholarship was specifically for young female entrepreneurs. She wrote a new essay, highlighting her entrepreneurial interests, and a few months later we got the call that she had won the Girls Going Places Entrepreneurial Scholarship...of $10,000. We were completely blown away. We knew then she had stumbled upon a winning formula for future scholarship essays.

At about that time, she began applying for college admissions. She applied to eight colleges, hoping that one of them would grant her admission and perhaps offer her a scholarship.

Because she was homeschooled, I felt it necessary to prove she was worthy of being in college. I was concerned that without an outside authority, like in a traditional school, college admissions people might not trust her transcript and application. So, I put together a package including pictures, descriptions, essays, and more that showed she was more than just a GPA and an ACT score.

The first application Brandi mailed off was to a university that accepted applications year-round. The applicants just wrote in the date they planned to start school. A few days later, a representative from the school called to say the university had received her application but not the application fee and wanted to offer her full scholarship including tuition, room, board and books. I was in complete shock. I said, "You DO know she's a junior...?" He said, "Yes, ma'am. We'll wait for her."

Brandi sent her application package to one of the colleges before touring its campus. After arriving for a tour, we were seated in a conference room with several other families, and the person escorting us in asked the names of the students. When she got to Brandi she said, "Oh! You're the one..." Evidently my daughter's application package had made the rounds, and an impression.

At that point, I knew we had an application package that was working. Even though she had been offered a full ride to one school, we didn't want to rest on our laurels. I was still spending almost all my free time searching for scholarships, and my daughter was spending much of her time applying for them. (I asked her recently how many scholarships she thinks she applied for. Her answer was, "Probably 80. Or more.") In all, Brandi accepted seven scholarships ranging from $500 to $42,000 for a grand total of $97,000. It was a lot of work for what was often only a little money, but it was more than what we had before the process started.

In March of her senior year, it was time for Brandi to decide which of the eight schools she wanted to attend. Each of the schools had offered a scholarship of some kind, but some covered more than others. It was a tough decision, and the price tag wasn't the only factor. In the end, she ended up choosing my alma mater. It wasn't going to be a totally free-ride, but I assured her that there were ways she could make it work.

Once she had made her decision, she formally 'withdrew' the other applications to release scholarship funds as well as her place in the freshman class to other students. Not long afterward, we got a call from one of the private out-of-state schools she had turned down. They asked, "What can we do to get you to come here?" I was shocked. They proceeded to offer her absolutely everything you could think of, including waiving the out-of-state fee and an on-campus job! While grateful for the gesture, Brandi was steadfast in her choice.

Once in college, because her scholarships still didn't fully cover room, board, or books, Brandi worked on campus as a Resident Assistant, which paid for her dorm room and earned a paycheck to cover the rest of her expenses. She also received an additional scholarship while in her senior year of college.

Then, I sat in wonderment once again, this time as my daughter walked across the stage and was handed her very own diploma. Unlike me, she graduated with $2,000 to spare and went on to have her dream wedding at Walt Disney World just two months later.

Had she been paying for student loans, that dream would never have become a reality.

Less than two years after getting married, Brandi and my son-in-law paid off his car and student loans and were featured in Dave Ramsey's newsletter and radio show. They've also been able to take multiple vacation trips every year since their marriage. Not having student loan debt makes a lot of things possible. They are currently living a very happy, debt-free life with my "grand-puppy."

What about my other child, you ask? Well, I used the same formula for my son's college and scholarship applications, and a year after Brandi graduated, he started college with six scholarships totaling $85,000. Currently, Sean is in his senior year and has cash in the bank.

Since dropping our son off at college, my husband and I have been full-time RV-ing in a forty-two-foot motor home, traveling and exploring the United States. Affording this lifestyle would never have been possible had we been paying for our children's college education.

My kids didn't have to struggle for every penny the way I did. They never worried that their tuition check would bounce. They didn't have to take food out of the cafeteria to avoid starving on weekends. And I didn't have to slip a $20 bill in their hands to ensure they'd have a decent meal. Now, as they move forward with their lives, I can be sure that they have a much more solid financial foundation to build their futures on. They'll never have to question whether they can afford a magazine at the grocery store. And, God willing, they'll never have to be...

Poor as Church Mice.

Scan the QR Code to View our Video Interview with:

Denise Thomas

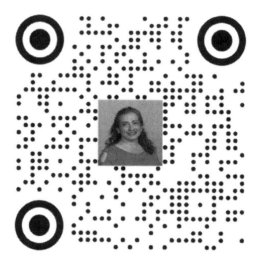

https://youtu.be/Hx6gYcTyPJs

Denise Thomas

From a starving college student who "lifted" food from her college campus cafeteria to have meals for the weekend, to an empty-nesting mom who figured out how to get colleges to beg her kids to attend their school, Denise Thomas has seen both famine and fortune.

Having homeschooled her two children from kindergarten through high school, Denise wasn't sure if colleges would have confidence in her 'mommy transcript' nor how her teens would pay for college. It was, for this reason, she created an application package that not only impressed admissions officers but had them begging for her teens to go to their school.

Both attended 4-year universities on $100,000 in scholarships and came out with cash. Denise has since coached parents of other college-bound teens for over 15 years, helping them achieve scholarships and admissions opportunities for their own children.

She is passionate about her work, which she conducts from an RV while exploring the U.S. full-time with her husband. Denise is the founder of Cracking the Code to FREE College.

To discover her high school to college method, contact Denise at **www.GetAheadOfTheClass.com**

Or, email **GetAheadOfTheClass@gmail.com**

Chapter 2

Let Go and Let God

By Darlene Coquerel

DEDICATION

I dedicate this chapter to God, because through Him all things are possible, and without HIM nothing matters. I've learned from Him not to store up my treasures on earth, where moth and rust destroy them, and thieves steal them; rather to store up my treasures in heaven because, where your treasures are, there also is your heart. [Matthew 6:19-20 NKJV] And, those treasures in heaven are all the souls that God has put in my path, whom I took the time to help during their time of need.

INTRODUCTION

My story has a recognizable theme, but the moral of my story is that, through adversity, change happens and that to let go and let God leads you right where you really want to be! So, sit back, relax, take deep breaths. As you feel compelled, put down the book, take a break, or write down what's in your heart. Continue reading when you feel led, because that is when you are vulnerable and receptive to God's word. Sometimes, it's a word of healing; sometimes, a word of wisdom; sometimes, His divine intervention.

Have you ever had a million-dollar idea come to you in the middle of the night? Or received an answer to something you've been stressing over for a long time? Do you know why that happens? It happens because your guard is down. Your conscious mind is not in the way, and your subconscious easily receives what you've been asking for all along. Ergo, the title: "Let Go and Let God!"

God gave us free will and created us in His own image, so we are intelligent beings. Unfortunately, sometimes we are too smart for our own good. Sometimes our pride prevents us from getting out of our own way and accepting the help we need.

MY STORY

I was born in Pittsburgh, Pennsylvania, where I spent the first twenty-two years of my life before a strange turn of events led me to Buffalo, New York. During the summer of 1983, my boyfriend became the Branch Manager for Encyclopedia Britannica at the amusement park, Darian Lake. As a condition of employment, he was to be given free accommodations in the RV park for the summer. That was the main reason we made the move. Our goal was to backpack the Appalachian Trail for six months, and we needed the free accommodations, so we could pay off the little debt that we had accrued.

Unfortunately, the deal fell through. We did not get free accommodations in the RV park, and we ended up renting an apartment, which killed our dream of paying off debt and spending six months on the Appalachian Trail.

During that summer, I also worked for Britannica, where I entered the world of sales for the first time under Britannica's amazing training. Until then, I had not been a salesperson, but I was a good student.

I studied the materials and memorized the presentation and the objections and rebuttals as I was instructed. For the next five years, I sold Encyclopedia Britannica. Years later, this played a crucial part in my success in real estate. In the meantime, my boyfriend moved to Las Vegas to work for the FBI and invited me to join him there. I wasn't ready for that, so we split up.

After two-and-a-half years of selling Encyclopedia Britannica in Buffalo, New York, I was offered a position managing the park information booth at Six Flags Over Georgia, selling encyclopedias to folks who were there with their families having fun. Talk about a difficult sell! I relocated to Atlanta, Georgia. Having never stepped foot in Atlanta prior to that move in March of 1986, I had no connections there except for my new manager.

That was the first day of the rest of my life. To this day, I am in Atlanta and loving it. But it was that strange sequence of events that led me here. Relocating to Atlanta was a God thing.

When I review the turning points of my life, I see so many times when God's divine intervention gently nudged me in a specific direction. Stormie Omartian wrote the book, *Just Enough Light for the Step I'm On*. It's about trusting God in the tough times. God knows that sometimes, if we knew what was ahead of us, we might not go on. Or we might choose a path that isn't in our best interest. During those times, we get just enough light for the step we are on.

That's what happened to me when I accepted the position to move to Atlanta. I had no idea what I was in for.

I started my job in March of 1986 and met the man who is now my ex in April of that year. He worked for Britannica in Atlanta and was a student in my training classes.

He left the company in July, when we started spending casual time together. We agreed that we weren't going to get involved, but then he stole a kiss. We got engaged in November and married in December. He was everything I had prayed for—a man who knew God and a man with high standards.

Fast forward to 1997. My husband and I attended a marriage retreat, and our assignment was to write a love letter to each other. For the first time in our marriage, he had difficulty writing a love letter to me. Up until then, he had always been the literary one, and I struggled to write well. I could write heart-felt words, but nothing fancy. In that retreat, for the first time, my husband used the "D" word. He said that when the kids grew up, he wanted to get a divorce!

What?! We were at a marriage retreat, openly expressing our issues, getting our love life back on tract, and he drops this bomb on me?! How was that possible?

We never know what is stewing under the surface with people around us. It turned out that my husband was in love with my best friend! Wow! Double whammy. I don't know what hurt more, my best friend's betrayal or my husband's. We were the last couple I ever expected this to happen to. How could he do this to me?

The two most important men in a woman's life are her father and her husband. I lost my father and my husband in the same month. On January 1, 1998, my husband left me and the children. On January 10, 1998, my father passed, having been diagnosed only three months earlier with stage four cancer in his stomach, his liver, and his colon.

My world fell apart. I was devastated. I was so stressed and emotionally upset that I couldn't leave the house. When I did go out, I would burst into tears at every sign that reminded me our marriage was over.

I was a single woman in Georgia and had no clue who I was. Eleven years after my move to Georgia and meeting "the man of my dreams," I was having an identity crisis! *Who am I?*

Every song, every TV show brought me to tears. There was nothing that didn't remind me of our marriage. I had done nothing to prepare for this. When I had said *'til death do us part,* I meant it.

Losing a spouse is as traumatizing as losing a loved one to death. The Bible says when God has joined the husband and wife together, they are no longer two, but one flesh. Divorce tears apart the flesh to make two again, and that tearing apart is painful. It felt like everything I had done for the betterment of the relationship was for naught. I've always believed that I could endure any trial or tribulation if I was secure on my home front, as long as my husband had my back. The world can be a hard place, and it helps to have someone watching your back.

That leads me to the moral of my story: *Look up, not around.* It took losing everything to gain my relationship with God. And that is when I learned to rely on God, not on others. I had to stop looking to others for answers.

FINDING GOD: A New Revelation

In 1999 I was on my face, devastated, defeated, nowhere to turn, and overwhelmed by it all. I had nothing left in me to fight, and my two daughters relied on me daily for their very existence. All I could do was cry.

One day while driving my daughters to elementary school, I passed by the Community Church outside of our neighborhood.

This was the very church where my ex-husband and I had attended that marriage retreat when he dropped the D-bomb.

My children had also gone there for Vacation Bible School during the summers, so I knew some folks there. But I had never ventured out of my comfort zone to be part of this church and community, even though it was within walking distance from my house. On this particular day, I stopped in to ask about counseling, because I was at the end of my rope with no resources and no idea how to turn the corner and pull myself out of it.

I introduced myself to the church secretary, Jeannine. I mentioned that my daughters attended Vacation Bible School there and that my husband and I had attended the marriage retreat a year ago.

She remembered me, and that gave me some comfort. Long story short, we ended my visit in prayer as I wept non-stop. Jeannine suggested I return for the women's prayer group. I said I would try.

Shortly thereafter, I started attending the prayer group and timidly joined in. One lady customarily broke into song during the prayer time, and I found it awkward at first. But I learned to look forward to those moments, as they brought me peace, they flushed my emotions, and I felt the courage to pray out loud. I later learned that people called this singing and praying *in the spirit*. It's another one of those *let go and let God* things.

I was at the church every time the doors were open, and it seemed all I did was cry and ask for prayer. I felt God leading me to linger at the church after services were over. I was so uncomfortable standing around and talking to people. I wanted to be invisible. I wanted to be at home alone and shut out the world. But I felt the word of God speaking to me, and through prayer I knew that I was supposed to be there, but I didn't know why.

I ended up volunteering in the café, where I got to know others. There I met an investor who became my bridge to move through that dark cloud in my life. I had been so depressed that I couldn't function, and I didn't even try to look for a job.

My agreement with my ex was that the real estate business we had built would support me and the girls. Unfortunately, that did not happen. I had to walk away from the business and let my ex keep it.

This was the turning point in my letting go of material things to gain a better understanding of what was more important in life!

I finally admitted that I couldn't handle it. I had to let go and let God show me the way out of this devastation. Once I surrendered, I gave my house away to an investor at my church the weekend before it was to go into foreclosure. The investor allowed me to stay on temporarily as a tenant until I could find another house, which took me an additional seven months. If I hadn't obediently kept attending the church and hanging around after service to get to know people, I would not have had the opportunity. My house would have gone into foreclosure, and I'd have had nowhere to go and no resources to get there.

God truly allows us to go through pain for the benefit of others at times. Had I not experienced foreclosure, I would not have known the process, and I would not have been able to empathize with and assist others going through it. Now I am an expert in all aspects of foreclosure, and it all started with my own adversity leading to the change I needed. It later became my cornerstone to building a successful real estate business. It is ironic (but no coincidence) that today my real estate business centers around foreclosures. I tell families in that situation that I am proof there is life on the other side.

I had to lose everything I knew to truly find God. As the Bible says, "It was in my weakness that His strength was made perfect." [II Corinthians 12:9 NKJV]. The stronger we are, the harder we fall. *The stronger we are, the harder it is to let go and let God.*

You see, God is a gentleman. He will never force himself on us. He gives us free will. He loves us no matter how self-serving we are or how much we stray from Him. *Free will.* Have you ever stopped to think about that? We set our own boundaries. We must be able to look up to God as our example. It's when we look around, instead of up, that we mess it up by saying things like, "I'm a good person. I'm a better person than that guy. Why should I be the one who must change? Why should I compromise?" All of this is self-centered thinking.

It's not until we finally take our eyes off ourselves that we can heal from the inside and become a better person. It's not until we lose our lives and focus on the bigger picture that we can experience our true potential and can influence others in unbelievable measures.

- Be the *you* that you want to be, and all the components of your life will come together. First you, then everything else will come together.

- Convince yourself that it's in the journey, not the destination.

- Your success comes in understanding your own journey. Tomorrow never becomes today. If you put off making a change in your way of thinking, expecting something different to happen tomorrow, you're already defeated.

- Ask yourself these questions:
  - What will I do today that makes me happy?
  - What will I do today that makes me successful?
  - What will I do today to make a difference in other people's lives?
  - What will I do today to live the dream that I've always dreamed of?
  - What will I do today to show my family that I love them?
  - What will I do for myself today?

My passion is helping others understand that no matter the circumstance that causes failure and pain, we must learn to "Flip the Script." Be introspective—look inward for answers. We cannot change anyone else. We can only change ourselves and how we react or respond in situations. When we are blindsided by the unimaginable, we freeze in our tracks, debilitated. We only want to shut out the world, curl into the fetal position, and not deal with it. Sometimes we think we want to die so it will all be over.

If you reach that point, you're ready to start your journey to recovery. That's when God shows you that He will never leave you, nor will He forsake you. Unfortunately, only you can take that necessary next step. Rest assured, years from now when all of this passes you will see this as one of the best things that ever happened to you.

I learned to change my focus from victimhood to healthy responsibility. You see, as a victim, we give ourselves permission to be a failure. We believe that we have no power to change our current situation. While there are external forces at play in our lives over which we have no control, believing that we can't do anything about it only makes us victims with no way out.

We must take control of our thoughts and our actions and accept responsibility for our actions. Ask yourself, "What is my responsibility here?" What does it take to Flip the Script? Society leads us to believe that we are victims of circumstance. What we need to learn is that, in spite of circumstances, we are in full control of our response. For example, if I am blind-sided by something someone does to me, my *own* actions must be considered for me to gain control over my outcome.

Flip the Script and tell yourself what outcome you want. Then let go and let God affect the change you want to happen.

Scan the QR code below to watch our video interview with:

Darlene Coquerel

https://youtu.be/DnmQ2EKWFFA

Darlene Coquerel is a real estate trainer and broker in multiple states. She has trained and coached real estate investors for more than 20 years and has a passion for building teams and helping people. Her current business model includes helping families facing foreclosure.

Using HUD's $100-down-payment program, Darlene purchased her first duplex in Lawrenceville, Georgia in 1991. In 1994, she obtained her real estate license to take her own investing business to the next level.

She joined the local Real Estate Investor's Association, where she studied with several coaches and networked and partnered with other investors who brought to the table elements of the deal that broadened her experience. She learned to do what she was good at and to delegate the rest. She teaches other investors to find their passion and stick with that!

Darlene is the author of real estate home study courses and books about buying and selling real estate. An instructor and mentor to real estate investors, she leads a local monthly Meetup group to help investors find and structure deals that get accepted. She coaches and trains for wholesaling, flipping, and buy-and-hold strategies.

In 2013, Darlene brokered a transaction of the largest number of single-family houses in history sold to one buyer for a total contract price of $105 million! In a 10-day contract, her team packaged and closed 1,367 houses to sell to Blackstone/Invitation Homes. She had acquired those houses over the previous 18 months while her team renovated them, placed tenants in them, and managed them prior to the sale. She went on to broker another 400 homes to Blackstone that same year.

In 2014, Darlene's brokerage was awarded the Platinum Investor Award by Auction.com, with acquisitions from Auction.com surpassing $75 million in one year!

As a national speaker, author, coach, mentor, and real estate JV partner, Darlene brings expertise and knowhow to the deal.

To find out if real estate investing is right for you, go to:

www.DarBuysHouses.com and click on FREE CONSULTATION to book an appointment. You can also visit Darlene here: **www.DarBuysHouses.com**

www.KDHRealty.com

https://www.facebook.com/darlene.coquerel

Chapter 3

No Mistakes

By Connie Queen

In life, there are no mistakes.

My daddy was an All-American football player, drafted by the Chicago Cardinals in 1953 (the year I was born). That event shaped the woman I am today. One of my favorite photographs is of me as a nine-month-old toddler wearing only a diaper, taking my very first steps while carrying Daddy's football. He was my hero, and I was the apple of his eye. Life was wonderful until my brother was born.

I was four years old when they brought him home from the hospital to our little red-brick house. My walls came tumbling down, and I shattered like Humpty Dumpty. For years to come, no matter how hard I competed for Daddy's affection, life was never the same.

Something changed. The football was now in the crib and out of my reach. Roles had been assigned. I was the "good little girl"—I was supposed to look pretty; say "yes, ma'am" and "yes, sir;" be seen and not heard; and, no matter what, act happy. *Happy?* How could I be happy when I was no longer number one?

Competition became my survival formula for life. I would show them. I would work hard and win. Then they would *have* to notice me. I would finally receive the love, approval, and validation I so desperately needed to feel okay.

One day in eighth grade, while I walked into P.E. class wearing the most atrocious gym suit ever, all I could see were the popular, gorgeous girls whose bodies were already developing. I was plagued by "comparinoia," comparing my insides to other people's outsides. My "rose-colored glasses" approach to life disappeared. My world turned dark and lonely, and the firm ground that had previously supported me turned into quicksand. Every day I slipped deeper and deeper below the surface, until I could barely breathe. I worked harder, studied more, stayed busy with outside activities, and stuffed my feelings until all I felt was NUMB!

I had no close friends. I crossed the street at the end of each school day to avoid the older girls' taunts. My family told me to put on a smile and to look for the light at the end of the tunnel. I assure you, the only light in my tunnel was from a freight train barreling down on me.

I ate to numb the pain. Daddy told me nobody loves a fat girl. That well-meaning comment made me feel even more isolated, and thus began many years of eating disorders. For the next twenty-five years I was on a diet; I was not on a diet; I binged, and I purged to maintain the perfect size.

The thinner I was, the more the boys seemed to like me. I even made cheerleader my senior year and represented South Arkansas in the Junior Miss state competition over Christmas break. In the spring of 1971, I was awarded a Junior Miss scholarship, I graduated with academic honors including recognition as Outstanding Girl Physical Education Student, and I accepted admission into the University of Alabama. Upon arrival, I pledged a sorority, set my sights on who I thought was the cutest boy on campus, and had my first drink of alcohol. I had arrived.

I was married at nineteen, bore two children, and was divorced (for the first time) by age twenty-six. My broken home and broken heart fanned my smoldering self-pity into a bonfire that fueled my reasons to have a drink and another and another. Between the ages of twenty-nine and forty-three, I tried everything. I remarried, moved thousands of miles away from Arkansas to Minnesota. I desperately endeavored to create an interest in different things in a new place among new people. Nothing worked. The more I tried to control life, the unhappier and more discontent I became.

Daddy died suddenly in August of 1994.

The next two years are a blur. I was heartsick, ashamed, and my fear bordered on panic. With husband number two and three kids in tow, I made another geographic move from the frigid temperatures to the desert sunshine of Arizona. No amount of heat could melt the chill within my soul. My marriage was on the rocks, we were on the verge of bankruptcy, and I could see no escape except for alcohol-induced oblivion. I wanted to die, and I had lost the courage to even take my own life.

I prayed for a miracle.

That spring, on the date of Daddy's birth, my miracle occurred. I crossed the threshold of my first ever twelve-step meeting.

I would like to tell you I stayed sober, but I didn't. I thought I had learned my lesson, but I was still confused. I married and divorced again within the fellowship of my twelve-step program. I was still incapable of forming a true relationship with another human being, and my effort to deal with life on life's terms led me back to drinking within twenty-seven months. Once again, my performance and accomplishments in life failed to measure up to my own expectations of myself.

Curled up in a fetal position, rocking myself back and forth on the cold bathroom tiles, uttering deep primal sounds from the depths of my anguished soul, I surrendered. In that moment, I acknowledged that God is either everything, or He is nothing. Either I was going to live, or I was going to die. What would I choose?

That defining moment comes to each of us at some point in our life—that ah-ha experience when the light bulb comes on, shining so brightly that it alters life forever. My game-changing moment came in the summer of 1998. I chose life. I chose to go to any length to have the life I am worthy and deserving of having. Was it easy?

No. Was it worth it? Absolutely!

Now, I wouldn't change a thing. What I thought was my deepest, darkest, most shameful secret turned out to be my biggest gift. I have immersed myself in learning everything I can about how to live my best life. I embraced the twelve steps with the fervor of a drowning victim without a life boat. I admitted personal powerlessness, acknowledged my mistakes and owned my assets, made restitution for harms done, and acted in service to my fellows, and as the result, I have had a spiritual awakening that put me on a pathway to peace and serenity. I've also had the great privilege to study with a few of the world's leading authorities on self-esteem, self-belief, and human potential.

What I learned as I pulled myself out of that deep, dark hole is that we all have our own version of *I'm not good enough* and

I'm unlovable. Now my truth is that I am not broken. I don't need to be fixed. I am perfectly imperfect exactly the way I am right here, right now. All I needed were the skills to rebuild my life and begin my journey to self-love and self-acceptance. My journey led me to obtain certification as a "Heal Your Life" workshop leader and life coach based on the philosophies of Louise Hay.

Prior to that time, I had spent my life complaining about what I perceived was missing or wrong, rather than being grateful for what I already had. I changed situations and circumstances to no avail, always ending up with the same results. Insanity! The "survival" tools that had brought me this far failed miserably. Navigating life with a set of made-up stories resembling the fairy tales of my childhood, about how I thought life *should* be, I had arrived at a place of disillusionment and greater loneliness than my soul had ever known.

I thought there was something innately wrong with me. I must be incapable of loving another person, or worse yet, I was unlovable and would never, ever, ever be happy. While participating in the Heal Your Life® Workshop Leader Certification course, I had a defining moment: Oh, my gosh! It wasn't *they* who needed to love me. It was *I* who needed to love me!

How and where was I to find love of my Self? The journey to love and happiness is an inside job. I had to change, but, what was I to do? First, I had to stop all criticism. Mirror work is a powerful technique for discovering negative, self-critical thoughts, learning to love and approve of myself, and taking grand steps forward in life. When I looked into my big, beautiful, bold brown eyes and said, "*I love you, Connie, I really, really, love you,*" cleansing, healing tears fell, and I connected with myself at an ever-deepening level.

For the first time in my life, I experienced the "twelve-inch drop." The distance from head to heart was the shortest distance of the longest journey of my life. Daily mirror work allows me to get out of my head and right into my heart and emotions. From that place of inner peace and contentment, I have limitless opportunities to live my best life.

It would be easy to continue to blame everything and everyone else for the emotional pain I endured. I was frustrated, struggling, sick, and suffering. An expression that rings true for me is, "Resentments are like taking poison and expecting the other person to die." Anger turned inward creates self-pity and depression, and it is a slow death.

The self-destruction that anger creates in all our relationships and in our body is insidious. These nasty little devils are hidden right below the surface, subconsciously sabotaging any chance at long-lasting happiness. I was blind to them.

We cannot change limiting beliefs unless we know what they are. People and circumstances, I realized, are mirrors for my healing. When I'm disturbed with people or situations, the spiritual axiom is that it's never about the other person. It's about what needs to be healed in me.

The good news is I am free! By uncovering the source of my discomfort and disturbance, I discovered the related causes and conditions and recovered a sense of peace and serenity. Now I forgive and make amends. My definition of forgiveness is giving up the right to punish myself and others for what I perceive was done or not done. I take corrective action when called for, and I am free. I am free from fear of people, of commitment, of failure, and of rejection. I am free to love and be loved. What a blessing! I finally stopped competing to win, and that allows everything I want to flow easily into my life.

I still had one huge obstacle to reframe in order to find love. I was familiar with marriage, but I lacked any knowledge about good relationships. I took hostages! In the past, what I sought in the next *Mr. Right Now* was based primarily on what had been missing from my most recent relationship. I focused on my complaints about "him" that bugged the crap out of me. Then I looked for someone who was "not that." All that got me was another one just like the other one. The insanity continued, because *not* is an invisible word. I still focused on the negative aspects of the previous relationship, which only attracted more of what I did NOT want. What a concept!

As I bewailed the sad state of my current affairs, my dearest friend had a novel idea. She suggested I write a list of the "10 Must Haves and 10 Can't Stands" that I sought in the ideal mate. "Good daters" carry a mental shopping list of traits they must have in a mate and traits they can't stand. My friend reminded me that dating is about "gathering information," not about finding someone to marry.

Seek wise counsel and pray about it—a lot and often. If a list is important for grocery shopping, it's a thousand times more important when you're shopping for a life partner. I sorted and sifted my likes and dislikes, preferences and aversions, and narrowed them down through a process of elimination. My goal was to have a list of twenty *non-negotiable* items.

Non-negotiable means non-negotiable! After making my list, I reported back to my friend with great pride and confidence in a job well done. Over hot lattes and after inviting God in, I revealed my heartfelt desires. She paused strategically for impact. Then she reviewed the list, placed her hand upon it, and slid it across the table to me. I'll always remember her exact words: "Now become that person. When you become a whole woman no longer competing with a man and expecting him to complete you, God will grace your life with a whole man to stand beside you. You will be two whole people coming together to create a third entity called a relationship, with God at the center."

I was speechless! What a concept! I spent the next five years doing exactly that.

Imagine my surprised when, in the winter of 2009, as my husband Ross and I were packing up our house in to retire in Mexico, I came across my list. It was at the bottom of my God Box. My husband was everything on my list—and, so was I!

Remarkable things, better than we could ever plan, come to us when we put ourselves in God's hands. By walking day by day on a path of spiritual progress, we live in a new and wonderful world, no matter what our present circumstances.

Do your mirror work, forgive yourself, make the list for whatever in life you DO want, and keep praying. There are no mistakes in life.

God has the PLAN! Comparison is the thief of all joy; so, stop competing. All you need are a few simple actions and to BELIEVE!

Scan the QR Code Below to Watch Our Video Interview with:

Connie Queen

https://youtu.be/0Zk8-91NhWM

Connie Queen, an international coach, author, mentor, and sports enthusiast, helps women in recovery claim their power, get in the game, and live an outrageously authentic life. As a catalyst for change, and through her own twenty-plus years of recovery, she works with women in harmony with traditional twelve-step communities to obtain and sustain true recovery in all aspects of life.

Through motivation, guidance, education, and spiritual practices, women break free from the shame, guilt, and embarrassment of living in the insanity of their dis-ease.

Connie is a game changer. She empowers women to choose a path that turns their inner critic into a cheer squad, excites their purpose, and reignites their energy and passion to create a vision that unlocks limitless potential. They go from merely surviving to absolutely thriving. Bottom line, they make their dreams a reality and they *Become Their Own #1 Fan*!

Chapter 4

Being Who I'm Becoming

By Christine Bennet-Clark

DEDICATION

With love and gratitude I dedicate this chapter to my daughter Serenity, son-in-law Chris, my four grandchildren Fenwick (Nick), Kira, Tasha and Rivers; my son Shane and his partner Sophie.

Being Who I'm Becoming

My life had turned into a grade B movie. Here I was at 58 years old, sneaking out of my apartment building, checking left and right, looking behind parked cars to make sure the repo man wasn't lurking, waiting to serve me with papers to tow my car away.

The threat of having my car repossessed was the least of my worries. I couldn't pay my rent and was in total fear of becoming a homeless bag lady.

How in the hell did this happen? How did I go from being a middle-class housewife to being on the verge of homelessness?

I was married for 25 years. Most of the time happily married. Or at least I thought so. I loved taking care of my husband and my daughter. We lived in the country, where I grew all our food, canning and freezing enough for us to use through the winter. Made dill pickles, green tomato pickles, zucchini pickles, sauerkraut, corn relish, canned over 100 quarts of tomatoes, and froze hundreds of bags of corn. Loved making lunches and taking them down to my hard-working husband at the grain elevator. I felt so blessed.

But it wasn't all roses. While I loved living in the country, I often felt very lonely and isolated. I didn't work out of the home, and I didn't have any real friends. Other than taking shopping trips into town, we didn't have a social life. Or at least, I didn't have a social life. My husband had a healthy social life with all the farmers that he worked with throughout the day. When he wasn't working, he didn't really want to socialize with his clients. My daughter had an active social life through her school activities and she work part-time.

My husband didn't want me to work. He always said it was for tax reasons. To him, it made more sense for me not to work so he could claim me as a tax deduction. I didn't really know about taxes and went along with it. At the time, I didn't know the huge price I was going to pay for my decision.

When my daughter graduated high school and left home, my husband and I moved to the small town of Vermilion, Alberta, then to Calgary, and finally to Winnipeg. I lost my connection with my purpose of being a wife and mother. I hadn't realized how much my garden meant to me in terms of feeling like I was contributing to the family. Just doing the housework wasn't enough for me. I wanted more. I wanted to do something. Be someone. Have something of my own.

My childhood dream had been to go to university, but I hadn't graduated from high school. Although I didn't enjoy living in the city much, it did offer me the opportunity to get my high school diploma through an adult education program. I then completed a Bachelor of Arts and started a Master's in adult education.

Being a student kept me busy, but I felt more and more disconnected from my life. I started feeling like I was going crazy. I often couldn't think straight, and my mind was fuzzy. Much later, I found out that I was suffering from the effects of hypothyroidism, which made me feel groggy and tired.

My husband and I were growing further and further apart. He wasn't happy with his job; it was very stressful, and he didn't enjoy the politics of big business. I still didn't have any friends other than my husband. So, when we started drifting apart, I came to feel more and more isolated.

The final blow to the marriage came when my husband was let go from his position as a result of a company merger. After that, he was at home all the time, and we didn't know how to adjust to this new relationship.

We survived another four years of increasing tension, stress and fighting. Finally, I'd had enough of the pain and suggested to my husband that we separate. He literally danced for joy.

We decided to stay in the same house until he bought another house. It was stressful to be living with a man I'd called my husband for 25 years but all of a sudden have no connection with him. Three days after we separated, he stayed out all night at a girlfriend's house. I felt incredibly betrayed. I couldn't believe he would do that while we were still under the same roof. I was so angry and ashamed that I asked him to move out immediately. And he did.

When he left, I was ecstatic, feeling absolutely free. I no longer had to worry about my husband's feelings or whether he was happy or not. I could focus on myself. Well, the ecstasy lasted about three minutes, until I realized that here I was, a 58-year-old woman with very little work experience, "too much" education, no job prospects and no money. There was less than $5,000 in the joint bank account. That's what I had to live on and pay all the household bills.

No job, no prospects, no income — what was I going to do?

Over the next several years, I spiraled down into a deep, deep depression born out of shame. I literally cried every day for a year. Probably longer. I was so tired of helping others; I wanted something for me. What was my purpose? I was meant for something more.

I'd always done for others — that had been my life. I only felt valued for what I did to help others. Reinforced by my mother's lifelong assertion that I was selfish, lazy and a quitter, I'd come to believe that I had very little intrinsic value.

In the meantime, I still had to pay the bills. I applied for many different jobs, with no success. So, I ended up renting out rooms in the house. At one point, there were six people living in different areas of my home, which was fine with me. What really surprised me was how easy I found living in a house full of strangers.

In 2010, three years after we had separated and sold the house, I moved back to the west coast, to White Rock, to take care of my aging mother. For a long time, I had wanted to move back to where I'd grown up, and this gave me the excuse to do so and to feel needed again.

Money was still an issue. I'd heard about people making money online, sometimes a lot of money. I thought, *How hard could it be?* Well, after years of studying and spending a ton of money, it turned out be a lot harder than it looked.

Two years later, I hadn't made any money at internet marketing, and I'd spent a lot of the money I'd received in my separation agreement. I'd never been good at managing money. Now, I found myself thinking, "Well, if this doesn't work, I can always kill myself." I was only half joking. Before moving back to the west coast, I had been fortunate enough to have the help of a very skilled therapist who had taught me how to deal with my suicidal thoughts through some very practical strategies that I still use. I think without her intervention, I would have taken my life.

That same year, in 2012, I went to Scottsdale, Arizona to attend an event for internet marketers. At the end of the first day, I was at the bar when a fellow attendee whom I'd never met or even seen before offered to buy me a drink. I accepted.

He then took me aside and said he often had visions about people and had come to accept that he should share these with the person, even if he didn't know them. He'd "seen" that I was suicidal, and he wanted me to know that there were many different versions of my life available to me, numerous life-paths leading to different futures. I was free to choose which life and future I wanted to have. While he was talking, I 'saw' those many versions of myself with different futures right there in front of me. It was so very real. I saw clearly that each one would lead to a different life, and that I only had to choose which one I wanted.

Although I accepted and believed what he had said, I wasn't able to get myself out of the suicidal thought pattern for many more years. If I hadn't needed to take care of my mother, I probably would have committed suicide. During the days and weeks and months after Mum transitioned in 2016, I felt even worse and more alone and more suicidal.

Money was my downfall. I sabotaged myself over and over again. I'd spent several years in and out of the courts, writing my own briefs to get a separation settlement; then I had recklessly spent it, leaving myself at risk of not being able to pay my rent. I even had to go to the local church to ask for help. I knew the minster, and she was kind enough to ask one of her parishioners for help. He graciously gave me more than enough money for the rent.

Feeling like such a failure only led to me become more suicidal. But I didn't learn from that experience. I sabotaged myself a second time. I had invested some of my separation money in two condos, which I rented out. When I sold them for more than $100,000 profit, I blew through the money, again putting myself at risk of homelessness. I had to borrow money from my children for rent, leading to more feelings of shame and failure.

What was going on? Why was I doing this to myself? Did I really want to live on the streets? Did I really want to kill myself?

One night, just before falling asleep, I had an out-of-body flash of watching myself writing suicide notes. This shook me to the core. I was truly afraid that I would make an irrevocable decision.

The experience jolted me into making a decision: either I wanted to live, or I wanted to die. Which was it going to be? At that moment, I decided that it was time to "sh-t or get off the pot," as the saying goes. Choose one and get serious about it.

All the while, I'd held that vision of the many versions of me that I could choose from. That night, I took a first step. I chose a version of myself that lives. From that day on, each morning, I wake up and make a choice about the new version of myself that I'm going to be. I've been *becoming who I am* without fear; I know the universe is holding me; I focus on setting my intention and leaving the outcome to the universe.

Since that night, I haven't thought about killing myself. Each day, I make a choice to do something that brings me further into a future of joy and abundance.

I faced a third month of not being able to pay my rent, but I was determined to find a way to earn the money through what I knew and what I'd learned as an internet marketer. Having set my intention, I quickly landed a contract and received a handsome first payment.

I've set a goal to never let my bank account go below a certain amount, more than enough to cover several months' worth of rental payments.

Something that really struck me when I divorced was how many, many women I met who were in the same situation I was. They'd been financially secure during their marriage but on divorce their financial situation declined to the extent that they too had become at risk of being homeless.

I did some research and found two studies that totally stunned me.

One study reported that while both the husband's and wife's incomes declined in the first two to three years after the divorce, the man's income returned to his pre-divorce income after three years and he continued to grow and prosper. On the other side, the wife's income not only dropped during the first three years after the divorce, it continued to drop in future years often taking them into poverty.

The second study was even more shocking.

High-level corporate women were asked what their biggest fear was. Surprisingly and shockingly they said it was their *fear of become a bag lady*. How can that be? Financially successful women at the top of their careers fear for their financial security.

Over years of taking internet marketing classes, I realized many internet marketers don't set up their online training in a way that allows them to measure the success of their students. I'd found a gap in the market. I created a measurable, step-by-step system to help companies get much better results for their students, clients and themselves. My colleagues have said repeatedly that I started glowing from the moment I put my foot on this path.

That was one of my first steps into my new life. Since finding those two studies my passion became helping women learn how to start an internet business that would make them financially independent by leveraging the power of the internet. I was adamant that all women, at whatever age and where ever they lived, should be financially independent.

I'd forgotten about that goal over the ensuing years of depression and my own struggle for survival. Having found my 'groove' again I'm back on track helping women build an online business they love. A business that gives them control over their own financial security and makes a massive impact in the lives of others.

It's not that I'm totally without the angst I've been carrying for years. What I have now is a clear vision of the life I want and know I can have. Helping others has always come naturally to me. The difference is now I am helping others achieve their goals while also achieving my own.

I hope my story will help others know that they too have many futures to choose from. And they too can step into the life they want and leave their old life behind. I'm not all the way to where I want to be, but each day, I take a step into a new version of myself that I'm becoming.

This new understanding was surprisingly confirmed in a recent training course with a mentor I admire and respect. He said, "If you don't like your current situation, all you have to do is make a choice to step into a new version of yourself. You don't have to heal or fix your current version. You can just step into a new version that doesn't have that illness or need to be fixed." Or, in my case, that doesn't feel shame or the need to self-sabotage.

That's what I'm doing every day. Stepping into a new version of myself. I'm **Being Who I'm Becoming.**

Scan the QR Code Below to Watch Our Video Interview with:

Christine Bennet-Clark

https://youtu.be/5QqfV_gFGnk

Christine Bennet-Clark is a West Coast-based, Client Success Consultant and Coach. She was born and raised in lower mainland British Columbia and has the privilege of living in almost every Canadian province where she had the opportunity to appreciate the diversity of Canada's landscape and people.

Christine was an early adopter of computers and online learning technology. She completed her Bachelor of Arts degree through distance learning at Athabasca University. She went on to complete a Master of Arts degree in adult education at the University of Calgary. Christine has presented her research on conflict in organizations in Canada and internationally in the United States and the United Kingdom.

At the age of 58, when most of her colleagues were thinking of retirement, Christine set off on a journey to learn internet marketing. With her knowledge, experience and skills in adult education it was an easy transition to helping entrepreneurs create online programs and businesses. She's become an accomplished internet marketing business coach, teaching clients how to build client acquisition funnels with her *Passion to Profits* and *Get Coaching Clients Online* programs.

Her goal is to help 1,000,000 women worldwide achieve financial independence by leveraging the power of the internet.

From her master's research study Christine was able to identify the elements of a winning program structure that leads to student success. Online entrepreneurs hire Christine to increase their client retention and renewal rates by showing them how to get student results that count.

Early mornings will usually find Christine walking on the beaches of White Rock, rain or shine. Christine loves to travel and there's no better destination than a visit with her four grandchildren.

To find out how you can create an online business connect with Christine:

E: cbennetc@gmail.com

FB Private Message Christine at:

www.facebook.com/christine.bennetclark

Join Christine's Free Digital Business Training Group – Fempreneurs Go Big Online:

https://www.facebook.com/groups/168573367419362/

www.linkedin.com/in/christine-bennet-clark-2a023721

Chapter 5

Wisdom Resides in the Body

By Kerry Cadambi

"Nothing ever goes away until it has taught us what we need to know."

Pema Chodron

Early afternoon on a spring day, my suburban Portland home was quiet. My husband of ten years was at work, and our young children were at school. I went upstairs, climbed into bed, and lay under the covers, alone and exhausted. I felt lost, deeply unsatisfied with my life, hopeless, and sad. I felt relieved to be alone to express and process my feelings.

Lying on my left side, clutching the pillow to my head, I cried. I cried buckets. Between the buckets were moments of quiet desolation. In that quiet I lay still, physically exhausted and emotionally drained, questioning.

Why did I have no energy? I could only climb stairs by taking to hands and knees. I couldn't stand on my feet to cook a meal without taking seated breaks. I spent hours of each day lying motionless in bed.

Is this all there is to my life? My breathing slowed, and in the quiet I listened to my heartbeat. It, too, slowed. I listened for each beat, aware of its rhythm in my chest. My breath slowed, and my heartbeats became further apart. *Did I just miss a beat? Is my heartbeat irregular?*

Then I wondered: *What would it be like if my heart stopped beating, if I just stopped breathing? What would it be like to stop existing?*

I wasn't suicidal. I didn't WANT to die. But I couldn't help but wonder if this was it. What if this was the end? I was at the bottom of my barrel; I felt exhausted, hopeless, and helpless. Empty.

In that moment I felt a sort of surrender, but to what I didn't exactly know. Maybe I was surrendering the belief that I knew it all, that I could power through anything all by myself.

I believe this surrender opened my receptivity to learning new ways to heal.

A Pretty Good Life

I had a pretty good life and plenty to live for. I grew up in a middle-class family with a good work ethic. My Dad told me, "You can have anything you want; you just have to work hard for it." I internalized that message.

I bought my first new bike with summer money earned picking strawberries. I bought clothes, shoes, and fabric with my babysitting earnings and paid my way to summer camps. I waitressed to save money for my airline ticket to spend a year as a Rotary Exchange Student in southern Brazil. I worked my way through college, and upon graduation, I immediately began working in the corporate world. I was an intelligent, strong woman who, by herself and with sheer determination, could power through anything.

I finished college and later met and married a man who also had a good work ethic and strong family values. After five years of marriage, we decided to start a family. Due to the nature of both our jobs, we thought it best that I stay home to raise the children.

For the next several years, I focused entirely on the care of our family and home. I knew that staying home to raise our lovely children was an important job, but I felt that society didn't place much value in it. In my first two years of momhood, when new acquaintances asked, "What do you do?" I responded, "I'm a stay-at-home Mom."

Sometimes that ended the conversation, as if they thought I didn't have enough brain for an intelligent conversation. I felt like a loser.

I spent my days cooking, cleaning, caring for the children, and generally taking care of our home and yard. To some degree, I enjoyed it and was grateful we had this option. But on a deeper level, it was unfulfilling.

There were no accolades for a job well done, no sense of accomplishment for work that is never done. I was externally oriented, focusing all my attention outward. My life was all about taking care of others. I had forgotten how to care for myself. To make it worse, I believed that self-care was selfish. I didn't indulge in things like mani-pedis, going out with girlfriends, taking classes, or going on retreats. On the outside, my life appeared to be going well.

And then it started unraveling.

The Mind/Body Connection

I remember the day that I stopped talking to my dad. My sister and her boyfriend had come into town to visit. My youngest child had not yet started school and was upstairs napping while I talked with them in the living room. "We're engaged!" she happily announced. "The wedding will be in October."

She picked up the phone to call Dad and share the good news. Animated and bubbly, she told him of her engagement, but his response disheartened her. Crestfallen, she hung up the phone. "What happened?" I asked. Dad's response to her happy announcement was, "I don't have time to go to the wedding." My sister was heartbroken, and I was angry! I never confronted my father about this, and I didn't speak with him for the next eight months.

My next contact with Dad was when my grandmother required open heart surgery. Only after I called her care facility did I learn she had been in the hospital for three days. Dad hadn't bothered to tell me.

I visited Grandma in the hospital and learned she would have open-heart surgery the next day. I spent time with her in the ICU after surgery, but early the next morning, ICU called to say she wouldn't last much longer. She passed just before I arrived at the hospital. I sat with her body until Dad showed up. I gave him space to see her, but afterward he was unwilling to engage in conversation about her funeral or accept my offer to help.

Again, Dad distanced himself from me and my siblings, not telling us when or where Grandmother's funeral would be. A great-uncle provided us the funeral details. We attended together, only to be ignored by our father. My anger at him heightened. Yet again, I did not confront him with my thoughts and feelings.

Three months later, at ten o'clock at night, I received a phone call from my step-mother. "Your father was murdered, and I thought you should know, since it will be on the ten o'clock news tonight."

I was shocked and devastated to learn that he had been stabbed in the heart at five o'clock that evening, and he had died instantly. It was the result of a thoughtless altercation between an inebriated parking-lot attendant and my Dad, who felt the rules didn't apply to him. Dad choked the attendant, whose attempt at self-defense proved unexpectedly deadly. Not only was I in shock, but now I had no way to bring resolution to our relationship. I could never tell him how his behavior affected me and how I felt. Anger, grief, and sadness churned within me. Before long, my health began a downhill slide.

Fast forward several months. I was tired all the time, and I didn't know why. The doctor who tested my thyroid levels announced, "Your TSH and T4 levels are within range. The thyroid looks fine." I had no energy, and they had no answers. An ENT physician, after looking in my throat, recommended I have my tonsils removed.

They put me on steroids, but to no good effect. I was more and more exhausted, unable to climb stairs except on my hands and knees. I spent a LOT of time in bed, in a maelstrom of emotions including depression.

One day as I lay in bed in the middle of the day, crying and feeling helpless and hopeless, I thought about my dad. I was still so very angry with him, even months after his death. In that moment, I actually spoke out loud: "I will never forgive him."

In the quiet moment that followed, I heard a small voice say, "By not forgiving him, you only poison yourself." *What?* I hadn't thought of that, but in my heart, it felt true.

Okay, for my own good, I needed to find my way to forgiveness. I would have to change my mind and change my thoughts. I listened to that small voice (at the time not stopping to think where it came from) to find a way to heal through forgiveness. Having reached a place of surrender, I was open to new ways to heal. Thus, began my path of exploration and discovery, my journey to heal my body, mind, emotions, and spirit.

A Path to Healing

Physical

I wish I could say my path to healing was "one and done," but no. I searched for alternative healing modalities. A naturopath worked to heal my adrenals and thyroid. I received Reiki, acupuncture, functional medicine, and applied kinesiology. All of this helped me heal on a physical level.

Mental

I read *You Can Heal Your Life* by Louise Hay—my first introduction to the idea that the thoughts we think and the words we speak create our experiences. It was my first understanding of the mind-body connection. I realized that my throat issues could be related to not speaking my truth, to holding back my words, not only with my father but in other relationships, too. I received counseling, which helped me to speak my needs in relationships, to engage in self-care, and to feel okay doing something just for me.

Emotional

I returned to school to train for a new career. I enjoyed the freedom of creative expression and the community of other students and professors. It fed me, energized me, and made me happy.

Spiritual

I took Reiki classes, and I traveled to the Casa healing center of John of God in Brazil. There I began working on my personal growth and spiritual development in an intentional way. I meditated daily to quiet my mind and connect to the deeper, wiser part of myself. I learned to trust my intuition. I was healing on an emotional level.

I sought out spiritual teachings. I read *Journey of Souls* by Michael Newton. Guess what: We are spirit having a human experience! I learned about reincarnation and the plans we make before incarnating.

Life was making more sense to me. I began attending church and, later, a spiritual center. I read more and more and had deep conversations with dear, like-minded friends. I learned we can receive guidance from loving Spirits on the "other side." I learned how to communicate with Spirit, and there are so many ways! At first, I asked for help finding parking spots; then I used a pendulum or Tarot cards for answers; and, finally, I did channeled writings. We all have guides, and they are willing and able to help us if we only ask. I understand now that Spirit has my back! And so, I continue my healing path of spiritual development.

One book I read suggested that healing begins with learning to love yourself. I began to practice that. The more I came to deeply love and accept myself and my body, the less I judged myself.

Consequently, I became less judgmental of others as well. Who would have thought that possible?

What I Now Know

I've learned that loving myself is the foundation that supports everything else in my life. I understand now that I must take care of myself before I can be available for others. Loving myself means listening to what my body tells me it needs—physically, mentally, emotionally, and spiritually. Self-care is NOT self-ish. It is of prime importance. Self-care leads to better energy management. I'm becoming healthier and feeling better, even as I grow older. On one of my dozen trips to John of God's Casa healing center in Brazil, I learned that we can only love another to the degree that we love ourselves. Greater self-love leads to greater capacity to love others.

I now experience how my thoughts and beliefs affect my health and my life experience. When I have out-of-balance moments, like an irrational emotional state or feeling stuck, blocked, or afraid, I work to discover the root cause and process it. Reveal it and heal it.

Sometimes I can do this work myself; other times I need the help of a professional. The more personal growth and healing work I do, the more I maintain a grounded, calm, and loving state of being.

But I am human, and the work is ongoing.

Through my study of Spiritism (the foundational writings of Allan Kardec) and practice of mediumship, I better understand what is at work in our universe. I can observe what is happening in our human world with greater equanimity. There are purposes for, and lessons learned from, all events and all interactions.

I know that we all have Spirit guides lovingly waiting to guide, teach, and help us. We are all mediums, to one degree or another. You don't have to be born special in order to have this divine connection. With assistance and practice, you can develop mediumship. I continue to work on strengthening my connection to Spirit. It is my go-to when I need wise and loving guidance and answers to pressing questions.

My divine Spirit guidance has helped me to understand my "soul purpose" in this incarnation and how to walk that path. My soul-purpose path defines my life direction, and I flow with greater ease. Rather than furiously paddling the canoe upstream against the current, I now float downstream, flowing with the current and nudging the paddles to gently correct course when necessary.

I am a lifelong learner, curious and eager to learn new things. I take great satisfaction in sharing what I have learned with others. I expect to keep learning, growing, and healing. I am grateful for the life I now live, for the loving connections I enjoy (both incarnate and discarnate), and for the direction they provide.

I now am driven to thrive—to live my soul purpose in this life, to continue my personal growth and healing work, and to help others lead a purpose-driven, soul-and spirit-connected life, with love and compassion toward all.

You, too, can walk the path to your better self through personal growth and mindfulness practices, understanding the mind-body connection, learning to love yourself, revealing and healing the parts that hold you back, and growing your connection to wise and loving guidance.

Go forth, be in peace, and practice love toward all.

The spirit is life, the mind the builder, and the body the result.

Edgar Cayce

Scan the QR Code Below to Watch Our Video Interview with:

Kerry Cadambi

https://youtu.be/Vnlp3mJRb0Q

I'm Kerry Cadambi, and here's how I was drawn to my calling in life:

Many years ago, a friend did a Reiki healing session for me. That experience was a major turning point in my life. It magnified my interest in the world of energy, spirit, and healing.

I have studied a variety of metaphysical and spiritual teachings. I am a certified Shiatsu massage therapist, and I am trained in the art of Reiki energy healing.

What I've noticed in my worldly travels is that so many people go about their days "firing on one engine." By that I mean they rely solely on what they can see and touch; they are unaware of the tremendous, untapped potential of Divine energy and intuition.

My journey of personal growth and transformation has been anything but straightforward. It took me more than twenty years of twisting and turning on life's rollercoaster to discover and embrace my true calling: to guide and support remarkable women to connect with their inner guidance and intuition.

All of my life's experiences — from health challenges to marital discord, from energy healing work to exploring past lives — have prepared me to live my life's purpose.

People easily open up to me. They feel safe with me. That's why I love to share this important work with people from all over the world.

"When I pass from the material world back into the purely spiritual world, I want to know that I've done what I came here to do and that I've helped others do the same."

As an avid gardener, I surround myself with the abundant beauty of nature. If you allow me into your world, I will show you how to plant, nurture, and grow the seeds of peace, transformation, and limitless, unfolding possibilities in the garden of your life.

Find Kerry at:

Website: https://www.thedivineguidancegift.com/

Email: Kerry@TheDivineGuidanceGift.com

Facebook: https://www.facebook.com/kerry.cadambi

Chapter 6

A Wise Woman's Journey

By Kyra Rosalind Lober

I like to say I danced on Broadway—in my mother's womb. My parents were in theater. I followed, in their footsteps, not on Broadway's commercial stages but as a concert artist and choreographer in contemporary dance.

Dancing and creating dances were my life. I received scholarships and grants supporting my studies and choreographic work. I choreographed for a number of dance companies. My group choreographies and solo concerts were also performed in museums, concert venues, and for TV in Canada and the U.S.A.

I was in my late twenties when the "Game Changer" of my life happened. The greatest stress I ever experienced hit suddenly then continued for what seemed like forever.

Just as I was receiving good reviews in *The New York Times*, I fell ill. At first, only my lower back was in pain. I thought it was an injury, but then other parts of my body were affected. Soon dancing became impossible. I tried anyway.

I remember one day I was taking a dance class when I had to stop. Another dancer's parents were sitting on the sidelines. They turned to me to say that I was the most beautiful dancer in this class of professionals.

This memory still touches my heart because I was feeling so vulnerable and helpless with my mysterious condition. That someone could see the beauty in me while I was so hurt seemed a miracle.

I couldn't fully take in that I was not well. I even managed to do several performances that I had booked prior to the onset of what I now know as an illness. Somehow, I danced though I could barely climb the stairs to exit the theater. I just would not give up.

I did not know what this was or why it was happening. It took a year before I had a diagnosis: throughout the year, I was seen by the world's top surgeons, chiropractors, and an array of alternative therapists. I finally went to a sports medicine doctor who connected the original pain in my back with the pains that had spread elsewhere. My hands and one knee were swollen. He sent me to a rheumatologist who tested my blood, poked and prodded me, then diagnosed rheumatoid arthritis with ankylosing spondylitis*. I was devastated.

The drug I was given by the doctor altered my consciousness to such an extent that I had a car accident backing out of a parking lot at less than one mile an hour. I had to find another way. However, at least, I knew the name of the physical aspect of my problem.

I saw a nutritionist from the well-known spiritual community, Findhorn, who said he wouldn't work with me unless I got off medication. I went cold turkey. This too was devastating. Any symptom alleviation I had experienced on the drug was completely reversed and the pain amplified. I could barely walk. The nutritionist realized that he had made a mistake: never take anyone off medication quickly without being aware of the potential consequences. Take it slow.

Still, I was lucky: the medical profession forgot to tell me that my condition was incurable. So, I was determined to get well. I never went back on the prescribed medication instead I explored natural therapies.

I had sessions in massage, CranioSacral Therapy, Acupuncture, Alexander Technique. Later I was fortunate to find Reiki, a non-invasive way of supporting one's bodily healing process. I met with psychologists: Jungian, Psychosynthesis, and Gestalt. I tried acupuncture (one wanted me to have several teeth pulled--weird, and I didn't do this!) I radically altered my diet, and this was helpful in the long run. I swallowed 25 vitamins at every meal. I fasted.

I resonated in particular with Psychosynthesis, the work of an Italian therapist, Roberto Assagioli. This process got in touch with my sub-personalities: the critic, dancer, little girl, adult and spiritual or higher self, to name a few. Aspects of me were in conflict with each other.

My exploration of psychology, therapists, and doctors had its ups and down. It was trial and error. A famous psychologist who had survived the holocaust told me dancing was childish. Basically, he denigrated who I was as a being.

Other therapists applied their techniques to me without listening to my body. I did not go back for their 'Pain is Gain' sessions. This is why light-touch therapies are my forte. Reiki, CranioSacral & Brain Therapy, Vibrational Acupuncture are a few of my specialties.

I did everything! It took me two and a half years to get well. At present, doctors would say that I'm in remission; indeed, I have been all of my life since then. My sister recently discovered that our DNA had a gene that makes us vulnerable to auto-immune diseases. So, I have an inherited stressor.

It was not, as you can gather, smooth sailing for those two and half years. The disease moved around in my body, affecting different parts in different ways. For instance, while I was studying somatic education far from home in Massachusetts, my eye became inflamed.

I went to the local emergency room and was misdiagnosed. I was given medication for pink eye, which did nothing. Sunlight was blinding. The pain was constant. Days later, I wound up at in ophthalmologist's office (an eye specialist).

He treated me for iritis, an inflammation of the colored part of the eye. I did not know it then, but iritis is associated with my illness, rheumatoid arthritis. The doctor had me come in to his office daily for three weeks as the pressure in my eye was so high. It still tears at my heart to realize that I could have lost my eyesight.

I was so unknowing of what was happening to me and so incredibly persistent in pursuing my wellness. Even today, if I have any issue with my eyes and I mention my history of iritis, I immediately get an appointment at any hospital eye clinic the next day, in Canada at least.

I also did a great deal of work on myself. When my hands were swollen with pain, I learned to juggle. I wound up juggling up to five balls at a time. I found play was often a better healer than exercise. I found toning (sending a humming sound) into the physical receptors or neuroendocrine glands of my Chakras (also known as energy centers) helped me to rebalance my hormones. I wasn't having regular menses at the time of my illness. As a dancer I always thought I was too heavy, but it seems I did not have enough weight on me to support hormonal balance and menstruation.

I waited every day for the window of opportunity that would take me out of my pain. Sometimes this would manifest through gentle play, free-form dance, meditation. Getting in touch with my repressed feelings was essential over this period. One of my meditations celebrated anger and ended in devotional dance. I had to do this one very gently or I would just hurt myself.

I also let go of everything and everyone in my life. I do not recommend this last approach.

One of the people I let go of was my wonderful husband. We got along super well, having phenomenal levels of respect for each other and our abilities. We collaborated on creative projects. The only time we argued was when we were in noisy environments. I have realized that noise is a trigger for me.

In many ways the relationship was the best gift I have ever given myself. Unfortunately, the chemistry of our initial love affair did not last. He and I also traveled separately for our work for as long as two months at a time, as my dancer parents had done when I was young.

And maybe we just got along too well. Something in my soul needed to work out my challenging younger years: parents who went away on tour with their shows leaving my care with other people. I later realized that this felt like abandonment to my younger self. Eventually my parents left each other, though they remained friends with unresolved issues to the very end, my mother's death some years ago.

It took me a long time to realize that everything appears inside of me; that my responses are my own responses to the situations that I am living. I may not have consciously caused a situation, but I am responsible for my response to it.

Changing relationships is not always the answer, looking

within is always helpful.

Dancing was my life. Initially the illness left me bereft of this essential aspect and purpose of my being. Expressing myself through dance allowed me to share my sense of beauty, my feelings, perceptions, and the joy of pure aliveness!

As I mentioned, I followed in my parents' footsteps; albeit, while they earned their living on the stage, in early television, Hollywood films, and even Las Vegas, I was involved in dance as an art form. I was a very serious artist expressing consciousness through the fluidity and structure of dance.

I also wanted to be technically perfect as a dancer; instead, I wound up feeling totally betrayed by my body. I realize now that I am a human being embodying spirit through my physical form. In fact, the body is spirit in form.

At that time, I was perhaps a tad over-attached to my young, beautiful body. I also wanted to be thinner. I am sure that I was just fine, but maybe all the dance classes I took looking in the mirror were not so great for 'being' in my body. Truth is almost always paradoxical. I was too attached to how I looked but also detached from experiencing many aspects of myself. Does this make sense? Have you experienced yourself as too much and too little at the same time?

Looking back, becoming ill with a chronic condition was the most significant event of my life. It changed the direction and purpose of my life.

What was and remains good is my commitment to realizing my full potential. Yet the stress I placed on myself then to continually create new choreography and perfect my art as a dancer was enormous. I also had personal issues that I was not so aware of at that time. Looking back, I see this period as the beginning of a refinement of who I am today and a major step on my journey to becoming a wiser woman.

What this period of my life taught me was to heal myself and prepared me to help others in healing themselves. I have assisted thousands to recover from chronic illness, acute pain, trauma, and anxiety.

I restructured my life at that time and I explored my spiritual path more deeply. I had many awakening experiences. This led me to perceive the world from a different perspective. I am not just a body. The body is the focal point of the now. The body has its reasons. It encompasses all of who we are, without being who we are in total. This is similar to understanding emotions are not all of who you are, yet express a part of you. Do remember if you have no body, you will have no emotions either, eh? And also, we store stuck emotions in the body.

During that time, I began training in the Body-Mind therapies that were at the forefront of an emerging field called Somatic Education.

This type of work often explores subtle aspects of consciousness and feeling through the body.

Much of it is based on the neurological foundation of human behavior. It ranges from the exploration of developmental movement patterns that children go through, from lying to sitting to standing and walking, to the very micro-movements of cells throughout the body and brain.

Taking the stress out doesn't mean throwing the baby out with the bath water, which I perhaps may have done. Our lives are about nurturing our life force and living our purpose while juggling the demands of work and family. Just remember that first love is self-love!

My life since then has focused on discovering unique paths to wellness. In Chinese medicine, stagnant Chi (energy) is considered to be the beginning of disease. You may have noticed that when you feel stressed, you feel stuck, probably especially stuck if you are pushing too hard as I did as a young dancer. We release stagnant Chi by discovering effective ways to cope with our stressors.

Today we are not only facing internal but increasing environmental stressors. The bottom line is how do we do minimize and/or eliminate their effects on us and by extension on those we love.

One other thing, doctors and surgeons are wonderful when you need them and great at diagnosing. But for chronic conditions, your best bet generally is to find natural solutions wherever possible.

Had I continued on medication, I would have suppressed the symptoms but never healed.

I recently Googled the long-term consequences of the drug I was originally given: gastric ulcers, GI bleeding, liver impairment, pancreatitis, colitis, convulsions, cardiac problems, severe skin changes, and mental status changes.

The 'natural way' for chronic conditions may take longer but is definitely worth it. On the other hand, taking medication for my eye condition saved my vision. It's always a matter of balance.

Letting go of stress in a drug-free, natural way is what I want to share with you in a new online program, DeStress for Success, Instant Relief for Working Women. The training itself is called Body Being & Heart: Wise Women Mastery. I offer you a number of different ways to de-stress and reframe your perception.

One path does not fit all but I am sure that you will find your needed approach in this training. These effective strategies are easy to incorporate into your life, whether your stress issue is mind, body or emotional—usually it is some of each. Body, mind, and feelings are connected.

I use my background as a dancer, therapist, and traveller on the Spiritual path to bring you Stress Relief. I have travelled the world on my non-religious Spiritual journey to come home to my Self! I have become the Wise Woman in my own journey and I encourage you to become the Wise Woman in your life.

I still dance for myself and sometimes for friends. This horrific illness, rheumatoid arthritis with ankylosing spondylitis, opened the door to my life as a therapist. I consider myself to be an artist in the field of touch: An Artist in Touch.

I integrate ancient wisdom with the newest Western therapeutic approaches. My Body Being & Heart system includes Cranio-Sacral Therapy, Vibrational Acupuncture, and Somatic Education as well as energetic and intuitive modalities such as Reiki and Chakra Balancing.

Learn more at my website https//bodybeingheart.com or feel free to e-mail me at **kyra@bodybeingheart.com**.

I should also mention that my mentoring sessions include long-distance healing.

Thank you for reading a part of my journey in becoming a

Wise Woman!

Never give up on Yourself!

Finally, I want to pass on a contemplative prayer shared with me by my beloved sister who spent her working life in the corporate world. It's a good, strong and powerful reminder of some of the ways we can let go and be less if not completely stress-free!

Welcoming Prayer

I let go of my desire for power and control — welcome, welcome, welcome.

I let go of my desire for esteem and affection — welcome, welcome, welcome.

I let go of my desire for safety and security — welcome, welcome, welcome.

I let go of my desire to change or cling to situations and experiences, and embrace them exactly as they are — welcome, welcome, welcome.

While doing all of the above, please remember You are Enough just as you are!

Sending Light & Love, Kyra

*Rheumatoid Arthritis is systemic and affects the whole-body system. It is in the blood unlike arthritis that affects older people with stiffness in certain joints.

Scan the QR Code below to watch our interview with:

Kyra Rosalind Lober

https://youtu.be/ssbRLz0quRA

Kyra Lober is the creator and director of the School for Body Being & Heart, Healing for Body & Spirit.

She has recently taught at the 43rd Annual SSF-IIHS, the Spiritual Science Fellowship, International Institute of Integral Human Sciences' International Conference: Living the Divine Potential, where Science Meets Spirituality.

Kyra is a certified Cranio-Sacral Therapist, a certified Teacher and Practitioner of Bonnie Cohen's Body-Mind Centering, certified Practitioner of Shiatsu and authorized teacher of Feldenkrais Awareness through Movement. She is also the creator of Vibrational Acupuncture based on Ken Koles' Unwinding the Meridians with Cranio-Sacral Therapy and Chinese Acupuncture Principles, Shiatsu and rebalancing energy with the nadii.

She is a Reiki Master, attuning others to the basics of hands-on energy healing. Kyra has a B.A. and M.A in Dance from the University of California at Los Angeles where she received a Rockefeller Foundation Grant and graduated from New York's High School of Performing Arts made famous in the movies 'Fame'. Kyra Lober is a spiritual teacher. She has travelled the world on her Spiritual journey and brings the insights and awareness of a lifetime to You!

Chapter 7

The In-Between Summer

By Kimberly Hobscheid

It was April, a beautiful time of the year in San Diego, California, as I drove away from my office to pick up my teenage son, Drew, from high school. The day was sunny and warm and filled with possibility. As an entrepreneur and the founder of the company, I am fortunate to be able to craft my schedule around important and fun activities in life, including connecting with my kid's mid-day when I pick them up from school.

My son was at the tail end of his high school sophomore year. Summer was around the bend. San Diego is chock full of delicious and interesting week-long camps to keep kids engaged, occupied, and entertained during the long summer break. Drew had sampled a wide variety of these camps over the years: learning at science camps at the Science Museum in Balboa Park; enjoying the waves of La Jolla during Surf Camp; going on a backstage tour of the San Diego Zoo at Zoo Camp, and splashing around at Sea World Camp.

A few summers back, he spent a week at "Bug Camp." He'd performed in plays with the Metropolitan Educational Theater program. He'd been a junior lifeguard in Del Mar, and he had spent two weeks on Catalina Island at Catalina Sea Camp learning to sail and kayak.

The Game Changer

This year was different. At fifteen, he felt too old for another year of summer camps. And it made sense. At five foot eleven, Drew was now taller than many of the counselors, and camps that had been joyous and fun now seemed a bit childish.

Summer for a fifteen-and-a-half-year-old is a time of transition. Drew was too old for another year of summer camps, but still a bit too young to land a summer job.

What was he to do with his time this summer?

Initially, we thought he could hang out with his older sister, Bridget, who would be home from college for the summer as well. The two of them could have taken a road trip together or enjoyed spending time catching up. Bridget could have taken Drew and his friends to the beach or to the local fairgrounds. But those possibilities came to a halt last week when we learned that Bridget, an environmental studies major, had landed a three-month dream internship on a sustainable ranch in Northern California. That meant she wouldn't be home until the end of the summer. And while everyone was thrilled for Bridget, Drew's chance for a fun, engaging, happy, and productive summer suddenly fell apart.

Drew and his sister are close. It was obvious he had been really looking forward to having her home. Now his outgoing, positive, charming personality was in the dumps. He spent the last several days after school sulking in his room and binge-watching Netflix. Was this the summer ahead of us? It looked pretty bleak.

As I drove to pick him up that afternoon, gloom weighed heavily on me.

He got in the car, and I mused about options. What could he do this summer? I hoped for something that would be fun and would keep him engaged and entertained. Something just right for his age that would give him some extra spending money. And, from my perspective, something that might look good on a college application, too!

I chatted with Drew as we drove, but he was not interested in even discussing it. I came up empty. When we got home, I did what any good parent does these days: I asked Google. I typed in "summer jobs for teens," and while Google offered plenty of interesting ideas, Drew was barely lukewarm about them.

Now, of course, there were the standard teen-centric suggestions: paper routes, babysitting, lawn mowing, and dog walking. There was even an app for dog owners to find dog walkers in their area, but frustratingly even that one had a minimum age requirement of eighteen. Sigh.

One creative idea required someone with a 3-D printer, which Drew happened to have. The position was a prototype service, printing out physical models for people who wanted to create prototype samples. Ten points for creative thinking! But that didn't appeal to Drew. Normally outgoing and creative, this year he was in a funk, shooting down each idea, one after the other. Too boring. Too ordinary. Too impossible. Eventually, he abandoned the conversation and went back to his room to do some homework and watch Netflix.

I totally got it. I was feeling frustrated on his behalf and felt like we were stuck. Drew had almost no interest at all in any of the ideas that were emerging. I needed a different approach.

I thought about his natural strengths. I thought about what he really enjoyed, what brought fun into his life. Drew is intrinsically extroverted. He is comfortable on stage, and his charming entertaining style. He has no trouble meeting and speaking to new people. He enjoys Drama at school and had secured the lead in some school plays. He was on the Improv team. Drew has a smooth, easy-to-listen-to voice, and he tells amazing stories that keep people entertained and listening for hours on end.

I started thinking about these natural strengths of his, and about what he really enjoyed doing when he had time to spare. As I added to this growing list of different skills and interests, a general picture started to form. I went back to Google, and as luck would have it I came across something that sounded like a strong possibility...narrating audiobooks.

Now, that seemed like a lot of fun! Not only for Drew, but for me as well! It was a wonderful blend of many of the things he enjoyed.

I did a little more research and gathered a list of equipment needed to create a home recording studio. Altogether, the items would cost about five hundred dollars. I stuck them in my Amazon cart for two-day delivery. Would Drew be interested, or would he toss out this next idea just like he did with the others? I decided that even if he wasn't interested, I was. I placed the order.

With Drew in a shoot-down-everything mood, I decided to hold off saying anything about it.

The weekend arrived, and we went about our day as usual. We had an event Saturday night in Balboa Park. During a break, I looked over the audiobook narrating sites again on my laptop. Drew was bored, and he asked to borrow my laptop to watch Netflix. I handed him the laptop, and the websites on creating audiobooks from home were front and center. He nudged me. "Hey, we can get paid for that?"

I smiled. A spark of interest! That was encouraging.

While Drew combed through the information, an alert popped up from Amazon that a package had been delivered to our home. He looked at me hopefully. I grinned and said there might be something interesting from Amazon on our porch when we got home. His face lit up as he asked: "Can we go home and get it now?"

I was thrilled. He was excited, interested, and on his way to fully engaged.

The box was at our door when we got back, and Drew happily set to opening it and looking through all of the new equipment. The box was filled with cool electronic components and shiny objects, including a beautiful large-diaphragm condenser microphone. An audio studio in a box!

But it was getting late, and I had already enjoyed a very full day. "Okay, it's bedtime for me. We can set this up in the morning, sweetheart." I said.

"So…where exactly were you thinking we would set it up?" asked Drew.

I smiled. "Well, rumor has it that a closet with no windows is the way to go. I was thinking the coat closet under the stairs. We could have a little room in there like Harry Potter."

I headed to bed, elated that he was excited and engaged in this new possibility.

Drew stayed up a while longer. The wheels were turning indeed!

When I came downstairs the next morning, he was beaming. Our coat closet had been transformed into a full-blown recording studio. Drew had hung old blankets on the walls for sound baffling, and he had set up and connected every piece of new equipment.

He'd brought in a small table and a chair. Each of the components—the microphone, stand, headphones, mixer, computer, cables, and more—had been carefully connected and tested. Apparently, he had watched a whole host of how-to videos on YouTube and our new setup was working beautifully.

Literally overnight, he had turned our coat closet into a professional recording studio.

Drew proudly gave me a tour and showed me that he had set up profiles for both of us as narrators on a website that connected narrators with authors. He had recorded, mastered, and uploaded a few samples for his profile. Not only that, he had submitted formal auditions for three books. His proud smile meant the world to me.

Drew was selected for and awarded two books within a matter of days, and I had begun auditioning as well. Our little production company was born. We completed our first two audiobooks about the same time, and we submitted them to Audible and Amazon. We were accepted for more books, and suddenly time was running short.

We had more business than we could handle. It was time for the next phase of this growing enterprise: managing time and production. We brainstormed about growing the business in other ways. Drew thought other people might like to learn how to become audiobook narrators and suggested we could teach a class on it. It sounded like a wonderful idea to me, so we pitched the idea to our local adult school and submitted a proposal. We included newly created bios and work samples. The program director at the adult school was immediately interested and it was entered into the catalog.

Our first class had eighteen people in it. The class was a hit, and the reviews raved about Drew's ability to teach and his dynamic personality. We were asked to come back and do more.

Meanwhile, friends and family and neighbors all asked about this new business. Many of them had books, but they had never thought about creating audiobooks from them.

We started connecting authors with the narrators we knew and a new model for our business began to form. In addition to producing audiobooks ourselves, we helped authors who didn't know how to get into the audiobook market by connecting them with narrators looking for work.

I created a website, and Drew promoted our emerging business over Instagram and other social media outlets. Turns out he is a boss on Instagram, which, up until then, I couldn't even spell.

This was not just a way to fill a summer. It was an opportunity to foster and grow a life-long love of entrepreneurship. It was a chance to instill an understanding of what it takes to be in business for yourself and to become successful, sustainable, and profitable. And it was an unparalleled opportunity for me to share with Drew the ins and outs of entrepreneurial business.

You see, for me, being an entrepreneur is an opportunity to create a lifestyle around what you love to do and how you can best serve others at the same time. This was a chance for Drew to feel what it was like to create something truly special.

The business has since grown. We have produced many audiobooks ourselves, and many more with other narrators. We work with authors and narrators around the world to create audiobooks from their published books. A number of our audiobooks have become bestsellers.

Drew, now nearly seventeen, has learned about creating a thriving business from an inkling of an idea and active interest. This experiment grew into an opportunity to share with him how to start and run a business. He learned how to read a profit-and-loss statement, how to plan for taxes. He learned what marketing is about. He learned how to manage risk, and how to promote and advertise. He learned the importance of customer service and reviews, references, and referrals, and he collected testimonials from clients to post on our website.

He learned about time management (homework comes first, then family time, then work) and the importance of momentum (do auditions for the next book before this one is finished, so there's something to look forward to).

For me, creating a business with my son and contributing to his learning and lifestyle was a gift unlike any other. I will cherish it forever. Whether Drew continues to grow it or moves onto something more interesting, it is an experience neither he nor I will never forget—an experience that broadened his horizons and gave him a taste of the sweetness of that life.

I learned something from all this as well. I learned that we are never too young...or too old...to be an entrepreneur.

Scan this QR Code to view our interview with:

Kimberly Hobscheid

https://youtu.be/0CH1krM47z4

Kimberly Hobscheid is a successful, best-selling audiobook producer. Her company, **I'm Hearing Stories**, publishes audiobooks and has helped countless authors at all levels to convert their books into audiobook format and distribute nationally and internationally.

Using her signature step-by-step program, she has helped both fiction and non-fiction authors create amazing audiobooks, access new markets, generate new business, and turn on the faucet for new streams of revenue in a consistent, reliable, and scalable model.

Kimberly's process gives them the freedom to enjoy it.

Kimberly is an adventurer, and has hiked sections of the Pacific Crest Trail, navigated Class IV rapids with one of Costa Rica's female Olympic medal-winning whitewater champions, sailed down the coast of Mexico on a 42-foot Yankee Clipper, and traversed two hundred miles on horseback through Canada's Jasper National Park.

Kimberly enjoys announcing at equestrian polo tournaments and has been a guest speaker in cities worldwide, inspiring people to get where they want to go.

Kimberly and her family currently live in San Diego, California, where the weather is sunny and 78 degrees.

Connect with Kimberly:

LinkedIn: www.linkedin.com/in/kimberlyhobscheid

Web: www.imhearingstories.com

Facebook: www.facebook.com/ImHearingStories

Instagram: https://instagram.com/imhearingstories/

Twitter: www.twitter.com/HearingStories

Contact: info@imhearingstories.com

Chapter 8

Pretending No More

By Kathleen Carlson

I was born fourth of six children, four boys and two girls, in an Italian/Irish Catholic home. We lived in the industrial area of a small town along the Ohio River. My father, his father, my uncles, my brother, and nearly every male in town worked in either the steel mills, the Paper Mill, or the coal mines. The jobs paid well, required hard work, and were NOT for females. In fact, if a female dared to apply—not that she had a chance of getting the job—she was seen as wanting to take "a man's job" away. If women "wanted to" or "had to" work, they could only do so as a waitress, a hospital worker, or a clerk at the mall. People were expected to play their clearly defined roles, and I felt increasingly limited and uncomfortable in those roles.

I would go on to play many roles in my life and to learn lessons from each of them—some good, some not so much, and some I would spend years to unlearn. My predominant, long-lasting role was that of the "Good Little Girl." You would recognize her in an instant; maybe you have even seen her in the mirror. I went to church, studied, got good grades, kept my room clean, and did whatever else I could to keep the spotlight off of me. This Good Little Girl did what she was told, when she was told. My brothers, however, did not, and their punishment was swift and harsh. I wanted none of that!

Being a Good Little Girl meant being seen and not heard. The summer I turned nine, my mom held our first-ever backyard party, weeds and all, to celebrate my brother's birthday on July 1st. Kids from the neighborhood came, tables were decorated and there were presents! And just a few days later, my aunt held a second party with the whole extended family, and they celebrated Allen too. Okay, maybe it was really a Fourth of July gathering that included a cake for Allen, but in my mind, it was his second birthday party. What a great year! I could not wait to see how I would be celebrated just eight days later, on my birthday.

I wasn't celebrated. In fact, no one even acknowledged it was my birthday until my godparents came to the door with a small cake and gift for me. I was running the vacuum and mom was cleaning. Everyone seemed uncomfortable and conversation was only small talk. "We thought you would be celebrating, so we just came over." My mom said, "Oh no, not today. I told Kathleen we will go shopping when..."(when hell froze over, actually). I could tell my mom was embarrassed, and it was awkward for everyone.

My aunt and uncle put the cake on the kitchen table, waited for me to open the gift, and then left. I just wanted to disappear and pretend it didn't happen. Having a bunch of brothers made that impossible, because after they left, my older brother laughed and made fun of me by singing "Happy Birthday" to me over and over. I did what I always did. I hid in my room alone and cried.

I was Mommy's little helper, and as cute as that sounds, it wasn't always by choice. We had an unspoken rule that if Mom was working, so was I. If my brothers and I were playing whiffle ball in the front yard and Mom started fixing dinner, I stopped playing whiffle ball and came in to set the table, make the salad, and do anything else a good sous chef would do. After dinner, of course, there were lots of dishes to do, and that was my job, too. I acted as assistant baker, laundromat attendant, and housekeeper.

My brothers had roles, too: they played football (both organized and in the hood), baseball (lots of baseball), and street basketball. To be fair, they took turns cutting the grass once a week, taking out the trash, occasionally shoveling snow, and (once a year) cleaning out the garage.

I learned to be a good helper, and that role continues to serve me well. But somewhere along the way, I took on the role of the Great Pretender as a self-preservation kind of thing. Pretending everything was okay allowed me to hide my real feelings, avoid embarrassment, save face, and avoid conflict. Pretending also allowed me to try on roles that I wasn't really ready for, and that gave me the time to grow into them.

Once when we were at our grandparents' house, I walked in on "Pap Pap" giving my brothers money. He handed Johnny a ten-dollar bill because he was older, and he gave Allen a five-dollar bill. And because I was standing there, wide-eyed and anticipating, he opened his wallet and begrudgingly handed me a single dollar bill. As if to read the question in my mind, he said, "Boys have to have money in their pocket." Going forward, I was careful to stay out of sight when the money was being dished out to avoid being embarrassed that I wanted some too. I pretended it didn't bother me, but it did. It still does.

All of us pretended things were okay at home, and we followed the "don't take family business to the street" rule. Truth is, behind those doors, things were mostly not okay. In fact, it was a chaotic mess. We kids were home alone together a lot, and collectively we didn't always make good choices. My mother worked nights as a waitress, and every day after work my father hung out at the Moose Lodge and drank. He and my mother fought often.

My bedroom was my only safe-haven amidst constant chaos, until I began to be molested on a regular basis. I was no longer safe anywhere in my own home. My daily crying became an annoyance, and my mother told me not to be such a cry baby. I learned never to cry in front of anyone.

This began the *everything is fine* phase of my life, and I perfected my great pretender persona.

My parents divorced when I was eleven. Despite his flaws, I loved my Dad, and to that point in my life, he was the only one who ever said right out loud that he loved me. Now he was leaving. Alone in my room, overlooking the driveway, I watched as my dad loaded up the trunk of his car with miscellaneous things to start his new life. I was heartbroken. I had no tools to deal with this pain, and I tried my hardest to disappear. As I heard him come up the basement stairs, I felt like a trapped rat. Where could I hide so that he wouldn't see my tears and feel my pain? He held me, and as he kissed me goodbye, he asked me to tell my mother that he loved her and that he always would.

I became good at problem-solving and decision-making, and I'd learned some handy survival skills. I had mastered hiding my emotions, and I totally subscribed to the "never let them see you sweat" sentiment.

A year later, my mother remarried and life stabilized. My stepfather was a good provider, and we had plenty of food in the house and no more nighttime battles. By the time I was thirteen, I was cleaning houses for neighbors and babysitting in the evenings. I liked not being at the mercy of someone else to give me money, and I loved making my own money, even if it was only fifty cents an hour!

Of all the things I learned in this environment, nothing was more ingrained than a good work ethic. My parents instilled in all of us the belief that if we could get on with a good company, work hard, and do everything we were asked to the best of our ability, that company would take care of us, and we would have a good future and good retirement. I didn't see my dad very often at all, but even as an adult, every conversation started with "Are you working good?"

When I was old enough, I got a job at the mall and quickly became the Assistant Manager at Jean Nicole, a women's clothing store.

Because I was a hard worker and a good manager, I got to travel to open new stores in Kentucky and other parts of Ohio. It was fun, and I learned lots of new skills. At nineteen, I became the manager of a new store sixty miles south of my hometown. Soon, the District Manager from The Gap recruited me away from Jean Nicole, and then the owners of Sydney's Designer Clothing lured me from The Gap. Each time, I made more money, and I felt better and better about myself. My new freedom made me realize I could live life on my own terms.

For as long as I remember, when I was hurt, embarrassed, or uncomfortable by other people's actions and decisions, I withdrew. I pretended it didn't matter or maybe even that I didn't notice what was happening. It was easier to pretend I didn't notice.

Until it wasn't. I wanted more!

I began to understand that I would always be limited in this area of the country, where women could only do what men would allow. And I began to challenge the thought that you can only earn what someone is willing to give you. So, at the age of twenty-one, with eight hundred dollars to my name, no credit cards, and no cell phone (they didn't exist yet), I made a new start. That September, I hooked up a small U-Haul on the back of my Ford Mustang with all my possessions, and together with Maggie, my cocker spaniel pup, I drove twenty-two hundred miles west to embrace the land of opportunity.

Job one was to find a company that would take care of me in exchange for my hard work.

Well, that worked out for a while. I led with my strongest skills — hard work, willingness to learn, and openness to possibilities. I landed a job with a Fortune 500 company. Check! However, I also worked part-time as a night cashier, and I worked two other jobs to cover my share of the rent for the apartment I shared with a stranger. I slept in a sleeping bag on the floor for the next six months.

Nonetheless, I was on my way, and the stars were beginning to align! The age of diversity was born, and women were now being considered for jobs once reserved only for men. My company sought women to train and promote, and I fit the bill. I jumped at the chance for training.

The industry was tough, and I would have to work a lot harder than some women were willing or able to do. I would love to say I sailed through without any pitfalls or downsides, but that simply isn't true. Women in management positions were not readily accepted. The men I was now supervising literally called me "token." Men and women who were older than me or had been around longer challenged, "What do you know?"

My new fancy nametag was not enough to make me their leader. I would have to increase my skills and, as one boss told me often, "Take a bath in my thick skin cream" if I were to survive. I entered the training program along with three other females, and I was the only one who became Store Manager. The phrase "smart enough to do the job and dumb enough to take it" rang in my ears throughout the coming years.

I was clear that I wanted the job and the money that came with it. My salary as a new manager rivaled the good salary that the millworkers were paid, and I didn't have to get dirty or work nights. What started out as a limited choice looked to be working out.

But I would have to prove myself worthy over and over again. When I asked for my first vacation so that I could get married, my boss and the head of Human Resources reminded me that I had committed to the training and that getting pregnant would compromise that promise.

I wasn't pregnant; I simply wanted to get married. Almost all of the male managers I knew were married. Why was I being threatened for wanting to do the same?

Clearly, if I wanted to grow my career and my salary, I needed to protect myself. Men who did not buy into the idea that women should have this job scrutinized me and forced me to prove my value. One day, our Division President came to visit. He was very nice to me, but as he walked me around the fifty-thousand-square-foot building, he put his arm around me and told me the story he had told his own daughter: It would be better if I left these kinds of big jobs to my husband and just be happy at home. That left no doubt about how he felt about his company embracing the Diversity policy.

That little walk around the store ignited something in me to change my game. I was no longer a young girl willing to pretend I hadn't just been told I didn't belong, that I should not go for the big jobs reserved for only men, that I had to receive only what others were willing to give me or allow me to have. That didn't sit well with me. I made it my mission to be sure others would never feel the way I did that day.

My career with that company lasted more than three decades. My teams grew in size as my career grew from eighty to one hundred twenty, to more than two thousand employees. I now *represented* the company they worked for. My self-assigned responsibility was to keep each of those people gainfully employed, to take care of those who worked hard and gave their all, in exchange for a good life and a good retirement, just as I had all those years. And for the better part of twenty years, that was easy to do.

At some point, the lingo went from "sales and gain" to "increasing shareholder value." In time, I began to understand the significance in the verbiage. Our company, like so many others, had lost sight of the fact that people make the company. Priorities shifted to keeping the shareholders happy.

Don't get me wrong. I fully understand the need for company profits, and I prided myself on increasing sales and producing massive profits over the years. But as time went on, it was never enough. There was more and more pressure to produce. No one was safe. Fewer people were making it to retirement. Instead, the pressure forced many to leave due to illness, some passed away, and others simply quit.

I did my best to pretend all was well, but there was no fooling my body. Stress took a huge toll, and I, too, left, limping and sick.

Company priorities had shifted, and the care and compassion for the very people who grew that company from Fortune 500 to the Fortune 50 status disappeared.

Let's all stop pretending. Many companies are in crisis. One big company after another closes its doors, leaving more people out of work. The divide between young professionals in the workforce and the leadership of companies they serve is vast.

It's time to start anew with knowing that, no matter what business you are in or what products you sell, you are in the people business first. For companies to have long-term success, leaders and employees all must honor that truth.

I eventually managed to shake off my need to withdraw and hide. I have come to like the spotlight! In the interest of making people first again, I have created Straight Up Success Academy, and I dedicate this next chapter of my life to bridging the divide.

For more information, visit

www.StraightUpSuccessAcademy.com

Kathleen Carlson is a Bestselling International Co-author, Executive Consultant, speaker, coach, and facilitator with more than 30 years of leadership experience with a Fortune 50 Retailer. After retiring from a successful career, Kathleen created Straight Up Success Academy where she works with retail executives to turn their managers into powerful leaders.

Kathleen specializes in the soft skills required to build, lead, train and retain strong productive teams. Her passion for people and profits blend well with her philosophy that to be successful in today's very diverse and ever changing environment, leaders must understand and embrace the fact that, "Regardless of the business you think you are in, the products of services you deliver, you are in the people business first." Today Kathleen offers a wide range of customized coaching programs and services from individual coaching and group coaching, to webinars/seminars and keynote speeches.

Connect with Kathleen:

Kathleen@StraightUpExecutiveConsulting.com

LinkedIn: **https://bit.ly/2Cy3PHH**

Facebook: **https://bit.ly/2PR3Wlw**

Scan this QR Code to watch our Video Interview with:

Kathleen Carlson

https://youtu.be/Ohp_EJaMdF4

Chapter 9

The Testing of Your Faith

By Dale Schroeder

Dedicated to Carol, my best friend and wife of my life, and to my Heavenly Father who graciously gave her to me.

I've had a blessed life.

I grew up in a happy, healthy, secure home. My brother and I had loving, accessible, and sacrificial parents. To this day, they are still the best role model of "team" that I've ever seen. They worked well together on countless household projects and home improvements. They valued education and set us both up for success, not only by encouraging us to further our education, but also by funding it.

They told us, "Go as long as you want; we'll cover it."

In 1985, I married Carol, my high school sweetheart, after we'd dated for more than seven years. I'm not slow, and I didn't have cold feet; we simply got off to an early start as fourteen and fifteen-year-old sophomores in Algebra II. Such was the beginning of "Team US." We alternated between work and finishing college, Carol completing the fifth year of her physical therapy program while I got my graduate degree in counseling psychology.

After three years of marriage, we both graduated and achieved DINK status (double income, no kids). Life was good and a little more relaxed. We finally had discretionary resources and time that didn't include studying together in a library.

We agreed from the beginning that we really didn't want to have children, and we were firm on the matter. Friends and family became resigned to our stance on the "kid thing." We were simply content starting satisfying careers and being together.

I was approaching thirty (nearly eight years later) when I saw the cutest little blonde girl, probably five or six years old, a few rows ahead of us in church. God induced in me a change of heart about having children. Maybe it was time. Concurrently, I feared Carol would suffocate me with a pillow in my sleep if I mentioned my change of heart (or delirium). We'd gone a long time with not even an episodic review of the subject. I was excited (and relieved) to learn that she had felt the same nudge from God.

Three months later we were pregnant! Our daughter was born in 1993, beautiful, happy, and healthy. Despite a challenging season of cholic, she was an easy child. She even slept through the night after only a few short months. I was so grateful to be blessed with an amazing wife and wonderful new daughter.

Have you ever had such clarity about and appreciation for the abundance in your life that you stop in your tracks to be grateful? You actually count your blessings or, just thank God for it all?

Upon reflection, that very gratitude made us more aware, vigilant, and prayerful after the second time we became pregnant. We knew we were clearly blessed (and a little spoiled) by the ease of our first child. "God, just give us a repeat of the first one. Boy, girl, I don't care, but a carbon copy, if you don't mind."

Thursday, April 13, 1995, the day before Good Friday, Carol made an appointment with her OB/GYN to address questions and concerns about her changes and physical symptoms. She was feeling well enough that she sent me on to work and said she would call me to relay results after her appointment.

I vividly recall every detail about the moments that followed.

The hospital where I worked had festivities planned, and it was busier than usual with patients' families visiting over Easter weekend. I wore black slacks, a white shirt, and a new, never-before-worn black, white, and red patterned tie. The group that I led had just finished, and I made my way to the hospital cafeteria. Having built my signature, ginormous, pineapple-covered salad, I was leaving the salad bar when Carol called.

Our baby was probably already dead. We didn't know yet if Carol would need a D&C. Despite efforts to be calm on the phone, she was clearly shaken. I was in utter shock. Neither of us had ever before faced a loss even close to this, and certainly not together as a couple.

I dropped my salad, told a colleague what had happened, and raced to the doctor's office across town. I drove every bit of eighty miles per hour in a sixty-miles-per-hour zone on Loop 1604. If I got pulled over, maybe the officer could get me there faster. Who really cares at this point, right?

I prayed as fast and furiously as I drove. "God, please protect Carol. Please protect Carol." I was numb and terrified at once. The whole series of events felt surreal and in slow motion.

The twenty-three years that followed have done little to alter those memories. Though the powerlessness and disbelief have subsided, I'm still amazed how clear the details and sequences remain.

There had been what seemed like a wave of miscarriages at our church at that time. Several families were our friends. Couples supported each other, but some became guarded. Some would share news of a pregnancy only after two to three months had passed and they felt it was "safe." Those who hadn't experienced such a loss exhibited something akin to "survivor's guilt." The exuberance of introducing a new, healthy child in the midst of others suffering loss was awkward and painful.

On a Sunday only weeks earlier, as we exited the church parking lot, I was thinking about our friends who'd had a sudden miscarriage and felt absolutely sick for them. Turning right onto Huebner Road to go home, I remarked to Carol, "I just don't know how people get through that. I don't see how I could."

Now, only weeks later, it was us.

I made it to the doctor's office in one piece and met Carol. She expressed it all without saying a word. The doctor reiterated that we had lost the baby probably a short time before. Carol would not have to be admitted to a hospital and could go home, where her body would naturally abort our dead child.

Events unfolded as the doctor predicted, and we began to settle in with what had just happened. That Carol was safe and would be physically all right and that we'd be able to try again for another child in the future was comforting and reassuring. I could exhale a little in knowing that.

But how to break the news to everyone? We had little to offer in the way of an explanation, and most people offered their condolences, simply not knowing what else to say. It carried its own awkwardness and pain. Hanging up and calling the next person on our list was brutal. We relived the event with each retelling of our story.

Our church family mobilized a "meal train," and dinners were brought to our door for the next couple of weeks. Folks would drop off food, visit, laugh, cry, and pray with us. Those who had suffered through their own miscarriage experience could relate and support us, while others simply empathized, probably with some sense of foreboding that it could have been them (or still might be).

Carol's safety made it easier for me to begin processing my own thoughts.

For years, I had encouraged and challenged my patients to "think about your thinking." Feel the feelings, of course, but go to that deeper cognitive level to make real, lasting change.

Now it was my turn.

Clinically, I could say that I had experience addressing and processing a plethora of life's pains. In thirty years of professional practice, including ten years of inpatient psychiatric and substance abuse treatment, I've probably forgotten more horror stories than most people have even heard.

But this wasn't about knowledge and expertise and experience with others' pain. This was my own hurt. Our own hurt. We felt sick, confused, and exhausted. It's like the oxygen was suddenly removed from the room. We were gasping for air, perpetually trying to catch our breath.

I recalled the words to old hymns and praise songs routinely sung on Sunday mornings. They spoke of God's love, glory, and power; that as Lord over all, He moves in our lives according to His good will. As part of His will and ultimately for our good, He gives and blesses. But sometimes, He also takes away.

Have you ever wished that God's plan operated more like a buffet? That you could go down the line of offerings and simply pick and choose?

The "give" part of that is fine, but the "take away" business? That causes uncomfortable *why* questions. Knowing all of the right Sunday School answers doesn't stop the questioning: *Why us? Why now? Why after being even more prayerful this time?*

Faith isn't faith until you have no control over the outcome.

I've said and shared that concept countless times with my patients. But wow, suddenly this was more personal and more difficult. My faith includes belief in certain doctrinal truths, including God's omniscience, sovereignty, and providence. That God is omniscient means that He already knows everything: past, present, and future. Sovereignty refers to His control over His universe and creation. I could handle those doctrines just fine, but providence was a stretch. Providence states that God is actively involved in His creation and directs events and circumstances to accomplish His own purposes. He doesn't simply spin the big marble, set it in motion, and walk away as if, "My work is done here; let's see what happens next."

His Word says that He, "Causes all things to work together for the good for those who love Him and are called according to His purpose" (Romans 8:28, NASB). For me, the personal struggle began when I tried to reconcile the "take away" part and the "working it all out" ultimately for the good. Oh, and that He is actively involved and directing it all.

When have you wrestled with *why* questions or tried to imagine something positive coming from your loss or tragedy?

Wrestling with my faith coincided with support that came from others. My greatest struggle was interacting with Christian co-workers who were also licensed, trained professionals. Though inside I knew that they really meant well and intended to be supportive, I became increasingly intolerant of the religious platitudes.

Maybe you've heard similar things and possibly even shared some of my strong, internal responses.

"God has a child waiting for you in Heaven." [That's gold! Wait, let me write that one down.]

"Sometimes there's this thing that happens called a blighted ovum, and that causes…." [Fascinating. And that helps me how?]

"We have to put the past behind and move forward." [It was only two weeks ago! Idiot. I mean, Brother/Sister idiot.]

And my personal favorite:

"Sometimes God allows things to happen because of things that we're not dealing with in our lives." [I want to hit you.] That's Christian code for "your sin caused that." The theology of that aside, it's a stupid thing to say to someone in response to a great loss.

Those first few weeks after I returned to work were the most difficult for me. Now I was not only grieving and trying to make sense of our loss spiritually, but I was also mad. The people who were trained and should know better happened to be the ones that I most wanted to "lay hands on," preferably around their necks.

God wired me as a process guy, to see the forest and the trees and be able to navigate between both. Even my clinical orientation was built around a systemic family therapy model: to be able to recognize, predict, and intervene in unhealthy patterns and choices and behaviors; to be able to connect the dots and intervene in people's stories and for their good.

God, in His love and grace, began to work in my life and in my recovery in ways that made "systemic sense." The heaviness started to feel lighter, and we moved from devastated to disappointed. The air slowly came back into the room, and we could emotionally breathe again.

God sent friends and even hospital inpatients to meet me in my place of healing. He used the very course that I taught at the time to walk me (alongside others) through a section dealing with how life events can cause a crisis of belief in our faith and how to refocus on how God might be working even through that crisis.

"Consider it all joy, my brethren, when you encounter various trials, knowing that the testing of your faith produces endurance." (James 1: 2-3, NASB)

That does not mean that I am supposed to have a great feeling of joy *about* my trial. The trial or struggle or life event itself is not joyful at all. It may be devastatingly painful. It is not about a disregard of feelings or some "holy denial." Rather, it is about being able to acknowledge those feelings and faithfully look beyond them.

What it does mean is that there is a greater purpose for that trial or struggle. God can use the pain from those experiences to grow our faith so that we might become more resolute and steadfast.

The uncertainty of my *why* gave way to the assurance of just believing Him. *Why* it happened became more about *that* He is in control. Because He's "got this," I can let go.

But my journey and growth during this season was not over. More change was born out of loss to come.

God took me to another crisis-of-belief situation and showed me how something from our tragedy could contribute to our future good and to the growth of my faith and trust in Him.

In the summer of 1997, we learned that our local hospital program, along with other units in Texas and throughout the country, would close before the end of the year. Contracts with hosting hospitals were changing, and we would very likely become "homeless." We heard rumblings throughout the summer and into the fall, and then it became official. Our last day would be the Wednesday before Thanksgiving Day.

Nice, right?

We received our pink slips in the mail a day or two before that Wednesday. I felt the way I had when I had gone boating with a friend and the boat sank out from under us — literally. The wind had stirred up the waves, and water flooded over the sides of the little flat-bottom boat.

I could swim well enough to save myself, and we both wore life jackets, but still! Boats aren't supposed to sink. They are supposed to be safe and secure. We had done nothing to jeopardize that.

That's how I felt when our program closed. Hospitals aren't supposed to close, certainly not in the '90's. They are big and institutional and unsinkable, right?

Our team gathered and lamented that our future probably would not be together. God spoke to me again—in terms that now even I could understand:

If I can get you through the loss of a child, do you not think that I can get you through the loss of this job?

I was immediately reminded of my words during my right-hand turn onto Huebner Road after church two years earlier. "I don't know how people get through this. I don't see how I could."

It's probably not cool (and not great for business) for a therapist to say he's hearing things, but it happened. I heard those words as clearly in my mind as if someone spoke them to my face.

And then, I knew. I knew that He was in control and had showed this "systems guy" how He would "work it all together for the good." That's no easy feat, as this systems guy is also a security guy. But He ultimately used several losses to demonstrate His faithfulness and grow my faith, while using my own words of disbelief.

It had never been my intention to go into private practice. Managed care swept through the insurance industry. Large groups were expected to flourish, and small practices were likely to struggle. It was a terrible time to begin a solo practice. But my hospital boat had sunk and challenged my definitions of security. I had already begun counseling several evenings a week and was contracted to do inpatient and outpatient work for our former competition. My private practice grew quickly, and a year later, I was a sole practitioner.

The loss of a child, the proof that He could get me through what I said I could not get through, the realized faith that also sustained me through a layoff, and His continued blessing my practice have all worked together to enable me to follow what I believe is to be my next path.

I've had the privilege of serving literally several thousand individuals, couples, and families in the last thirty years. It has, however, always been on the "back end." That is, I've entered people's stories *after* the problem appeared, and often, after years of their denial about it or their simple inability to fix it.

Those experiences rekindled in me a passion to serve Christian singles on the "front end" of relationship commitment. As a marriage and family therapist, I've seen countless couples struggle with unresolved conflicts, often born out of poor relationship fit or incompatibility from the beginning. Even shared faith is often (errantly) assumed to signal "good couple fit."

I would not dream so big or take such a leap of faith had God not showed me how He used my pain for good, not only in my personal life, but also in the lives of those I serve.

I've learned that He works and wants to be involved in those relational areas of our lives just as much as in our personal struggles, losses and pain.

I want singles to "know how to know" God's design for their relationships and to see how He works actively in and through those relationships to accomplish His greater purpose—for themselves, for their future partner, and for His glory.

I want them to have what I've had—the joy of marrying a true, life partner who is also a best friend.

In May of 1996, we welcomed our son into our family, three days short of three years after his sister was born and thirteen months after we lost our middle child. Like his sister, he was happy and healthy and a joy. On June 1, 2018, Carol and I celebrated thirty-three years of marriage together. I couldn't ask for a better friend and supportive life partner.

My black, white, and red patterned tie still rocks, and still hangs with all of my other ones. I've never worn it since that day in April of 1995—not because of the pain, but because of what it represents. It's like a retired athlete's jersey. It's simply just too sacred to wear.

I've had a blessed life.

Scan the QR Code below to view our interview with:

Dale Schroeder

https://youtu.be/psWUzqVUuCA

In 2018, Dale Schroeder celebrated 30 years in the field of psychotherapy, treating psychiatric and substance issues while working the gamut of continuum of care venues for mental health, including inpatient, day treatment, and outpatient programs. He practices in Texas as a...

- Licensed Professional Counselor Licensed Marriage & Family Therapist
- Licensed Chemical Dependency Counselor
- Certified Anger Resolution Therapist
- Certified Diplomate in Psychotherapy
- Certified Professional Counseling Educator
- Certified Clinical Faith-Based Counselor
- Certified Money Habitudes Coach

Dale is the founder of Schroeder Family Counseling and has been in full-time private practice since 1997, helping thousands of people achieve dramatic breakthroughs and lasting change in their personal lives and relationships. He is a facilitator for Couple Communication workshops and also practices as a relationship coach, specializing in Christian Singles Coaching through the Relationship Coaching Institute.

In 2018, he founded "Partners on Point", what he calls a faith-based, pre-commitment "edu-training" program for Christian singles. Dale's passion for singles grew out of a desire to help relationships on the "front end" of commitment, rather than only treating singles and couples during or after a crisis. He teaches Christian singles how to apply biblical principles in understanding the pitfalls and blind-spots in their dating practices, allowing them to *be certain before being committed.*

Dale is also a popular speaker to churches, businesses, and schools and the author of numerous articles and columns on mental health issues, counseling, and the family. He and his wife are very active at their local church where he has served as a Point Person, Deacon, and Elder.

He is the father of two adult children (both engineers!) and proudly claims no genetic contribution to any mathematic/physics abilities, instead crediting their brilliant mother. Dale resides with Carol, his lovely wife of 33 years, in San Antonio, TX.

Chapter 10

From Solitude to Sisterhood

By Kat Halushka

I stood on the ledge of the fourteenth floor of a downtown parking lot. I felt the wind on my skin. Street noise filled the air: cars driving below me, people walking. No, I wasn't going to jump. I just wanted to feel whole; I wanted to feel like I belonged.

Ten years ago, my parents emigrated from Russian to Canada in search of a better life and a brighter future for my brother and me. One beautiful fall morning, while I was getting ready for college, my mom came into the living room and announced, "All of the paperwork went through, we are moving to Canada." At that point, those words didn't even settle in. I didn't understand the full impact of what she said until we sold our apartment and booked the flights.

"We" decided it was best to leave right after my graduation from college. Mom said we could each take only one suitcase. *One suitcase? How am I going to fit nineteen years of my life into one suitcase?!* Sorting through every little possession to choose what to give up and leave behind was *hard*—my favorite book that I read so many times the cover is now taped to its spine; my cassette tapes that have been my best friends and companions through good times and bad; my first cell phone—I had to give that up, too.

Saying my goodbyes at the airport was the hardest. My

friends came to give me one last hug. I held it together pretty well as final goodbyes were said with hugs and kisses. Then we were shoved into the departure line, where time seemed to drag on forever.

That's when all hell broke loose. Through the next three flights and twenty-four hours of travel through customs and plane changes, I never stopped crying. None of us spoke enough English to even get directions to the next flight, never mind check on our dog, who was forced to travel in the undercarriage. We listened, helpless, as she howled on what felt like the longest flight of my life.

We landed in Canada, and I felt empty, as if I had left my soul, my whole being, behind. Now I was only a body — the empty shell of a person. I didn't really care what might happen from there.

Strangers picked us up from the airport and drove us to an empty apartment. It was dark, and I just watched the lights passing by, feeling more and more empty with every kilometer.

The apartment was smaller than the one we had in Russia. I didn't want to unpack. It didn't feel like home, so at every chance, I left. I wandered the streets, walking for hours. I would leave in the morning and come back late at night.

Meanwhile, my parents were worried sick. They worked so hard to rebuild our lives, to get a car, a house, jobs. None of it mattered to me. I felt empty and sick with grief over losing all my friends and missing my old life.

Don't get me wrong; I love my parents with my whole being. It might sound like I blamed them for ruining my life, and for the first year or so after moving to Canada, I did. It took some growth for me to realize that it's not something they did TO us, but rather FOR us. My parents were hit the hardest, taking on infinite responsibility, learning another language so late in life, all while taking care of two kids and a dog.

My mom is my inspiration. When we were younger, she did everything she could to be sure we had everything we needed and that we were happy. Sometimes it meant being a stay-at-home mom; sometimes she worked a job while taking care of me and my brother, and many times she scraped by with barely any sleep. When you meet my mom, you can almost SEE the love!

My dad is my main motivator in life, though. He is the reason for my incredible drive for success. When I was a kid, he worked to make sure we had food on the table and a roof over our head. He worked as a mechanic on tankers, and his job took him all around the world.

He would be away from the family for six months at a time, sometimes more. It was hard to explain to my friends that I even had a dad, when he was never around. I can't imagine being away from my friends and family for that long. So, growing up, I always wanted to live a life of location freedom, financial freedom, and time freedom. I wanted to be able to spend as much time as I want with people I care about and not have to worry about anything.

Eventually, I went through the motions of getting a job to help pay the bills. Seemed like the right thing to do. I took English As Second Language classes. I went back to college to get yet another diploma and, hopefully, a higher paying job. By then I had some friends. I had all the things you "should" accomplish in life. And I got used to Canada and all its weird quirks. Like asking, "How are ya?" and never actually expecting an answer or even caring about it. Like saying, "Hi," to strangers, and buying coffee at the drive-through instead of just making it at home.

But deep inside, I still felt empty. Something was missing.

You know that feeling that you are meant for something bigger, but you don't quite know what it is? And it keeps nagging at you: "Hello, I'm still here..."

That feeling brought me to the ledge of the fourteenth-floor parking lot where there was nothing but me and my thoughts. It wasn't my first time standing there. There was something pure about being on the edge of "the world" — my world. *Why do I feel out of place, anxious, like something is missing? I have everything I ever wanted — my own place, a car, friends who love me, a job that pays well. I even started a business. What else can I wish for?*

That week I came into the office as always at eight o'clock, and a thought stopped me in my tracks. I froze. "I'm wasting my life away." My manager snapped at me all the time, my co-workers were backstabbing b#@%s, there was nothing meaningful to do, and I feel like my passion for web development had been killed by so many useless projects of no impact.

I sat down at my desk, turned on the computer, and loaded the task management (which, again, was blank). I couldn't get out of my head: "I'm wasting my life away. I'm wasting my life away. I'm wasting my life away." My whole body was filled with regret. At that moment, I decided to quit. How could I not?! Staying on at this point would be a conscious decision to waste my life. I gave myself twenty-four hours to "sleep on it," meanwhile preparing my resignation letter and getting more and more excited. I had no savings, and I had no plan. I just knew I couldn't live like this anymore.

By the next morning, I had printed two copies of my resignation letter and requested a meeting with my manager first thing. I walked into his office and, before even saying anything, handed him my resignation letter, hands shaking. I sat down.

My manager smirked—another confirmation that I was doing the right thing for me. Women weren't taken seriously in this organization. "Guy talk" was prominent and obvious throughout the building. This wasn't the first job where I was treated differently just because I was a woman. I never let it get to me, but I knew that there was a better way to make money. A way where I wouldn't have to tolerate "guy talk," watch my boss ask one of the office girls to do the dishes, or see promotions go to the boss's drinking buddies.

Two weeks later I was done, ready to spread my wings. I didn't know what I wanted to do just yet. I only knew I had to replace my income while making a positive impact in this world.

On my drive home from the last day at my job, I wasn't sure what I felt. The tears would come on, and then I would laugh, giddy to be done with it. I was scared of what might come next. My emotions were playing Russian roulette. Have you ever felt like that?

Over the next few years, I started several businesses. I had a web design agency, a marketing agency (with a partner), and even a network marketing business. None of that felt like the right fit.

Those businesses helped me replace my income, but at what cost? I was working all the time and still didn't feel I was making the positive impact I so deeply desired. I got lost in the bills, client projects, and team management, pushing my search for purpose to the back burner. Soon I forgot why I had quit my job in the first place.

I dug deeper within me. Throughout my journey, I had discovered a passion for bringing people together and for teaching. When I was a kid, I always wanted to be a teacher. I admired my teachers in school and had huge respect for what they did. When I had an opportunity to do a few classes for the second graders, I loved every second of it. As many things do when you grow up, that passion and dream got lost somewhere between adulting, paying bills, and day-to-day challenges.

Now the passion was back — and I wasn't about to let it go!

With newly discovered and revived passions, I was unstoppable. I brought together thousands of people, helping them with everything from health to business. Public speaking became my second nature, from my own events to international stages all over the world. I came closer and closer to what it is I'm meant to create in this world.

It wasn't until two amazing ladies, Kimberly Carson-Richards and Susan Binnie, came into my life that I finally found THE ONE THING that lit me on fire, that made me feel like I belong and am serving my purpose! Ironically, I met these ladies at different times in my life, and even in different cities. One day, by chance, both were invited for a girls' night at my place, as I wanted to get to know them better. Not even five minutes into the night, we laughed so hard that we couldn't breathe. I knew then that they are my people, and that we will create something beautiful together — at the time I had no clue what that would be. That night we decided that girls' night would be a monthly thing! We all wanted more laughter in our lives.

The next month, we got together at Kim's place. It was a cool night in June, so we got cozy around the firepit in the backyard. We talked, laughed, and enjoyed each other's company. We talked about our lives and how our businesses fit into them.

We shared the struggles we had each experienced in past years and the massive amount of money we invested to become successful entrepreneurs. We talked about how difficult and lonely the life of an entrepreneur can be. We talked of our common passion for empowering others, one woman at a time.

What would it look like if we started a community where there is support, resources, and tools to help everyone succeed?

We imagined a sisterhood of women who could all learn what they need, when they need it, and be supported to fulfill their dreams. Could we create such a place to help women succeed in business and bring their vision to reality? A sacred space where women entrepreneurs can be vulnerable and have access to the tools and resources they require? What would we call this sisterhood? What would we include?

Ideas flowed, and before long we had a clear business model to help women all around the world to bring their business to the next level. We all want the million-dollar lifestyle, a successful, joyful, and profitable business to supply everything we want and need to live the life of our dreams.

The Million Dollar Sisterhood was born! We hit the ground running, and within two weeks we were enrolling Profit Sisters. The three of us coming together to collectively share our own areas of expertise has true power-power of the sisterhood!

Now, every single day, I wake up feeling aligned with my purpose and fired up to help Profit Sisters at Million Dollar Sisterhood take another step closer to their dreams. I get to travel the world and speak on international stages. My business partners are my best friends, and I couldn't wish for more.

And, that fourteenth floor of a downtown parking lot — I exchanged it for beaches in Maui and evenings with friends around a fire.

Do you feel you are living your life on purpose? If not, what is one step you can take today to move closer to living your life to its fullest?

To join the Free Million Dollar Sisterhood community, visit

http://milliondollarsisterhood.com/freegroup

To connect with Kat email **kat@milliondollarsisterhood.com**

Scan the QR Code below to view our interview with:

Kat Halushka

https://youtu.be/YPhcj7cJl4M

Million Dollar Coach -Kat Halushka

Kat Halushka is an international mentor, speaker and coach. After moving to Canada, she got another diploma, a house, built a 6-figure marketing agency from the ground up in less than a year. Shortly she realized that all these achievements didn't fill the emptiness within her. She knew there is more.

At age 32, Kat gathered her passion for community building with Kim and Susan to start a collaborative business with purpose in mine -Million Dollar Sisterhood. Her life forever changed. They built a space for women entrepreneurs to get all the support and tools they need to grow a business, as well as a community where they never have to feel alone. A sisterhood full of support, love and success.

To connect with Kat email **kat@milliondollarsisterhood.com** To join Free Million Dollar Sisterhood community, visit

http://milliondollarsisterhood.com/freegroup

Chapter 11

From Invisible Leader to International Speaker

By Justin James

I was the smart, nerdy kid — socially awkward, thick glasses, uncool Kmart clothes, and a bad haircut. I marched to my own beat, literally; I even played the drums. But I didn't fit in with either the nerdy kids or the musicians. I didn't like studying just for the sake of nerdy good grades, nor was I into drugs, drinking, and skipping school with the musicians.

Without a tribe, I became even more shy and introverted. It was safer to be a fly on the wall than to try to fit in and risk being ridiculed. Ironically, this made me look like a good listener. People complimented my listening skills, when in reality, I was just afraid to speak up.

In one-on-one conversations, though, I had no trouble speaking up. In fact, it was hard to make me stop talking. I am passionate, and I love to share my excitement with anyone who will listen. Early on, I envisioned being a teacher. But, due to my shy and introverted nature, I was terrible at sharing my knowledge in a way that was easy for others to consume and act upon. I could never stand in front of a group of people and be a successful teacher.

I had to find a different path. I knew this meant college, but I was so tired of school by the time I graduated high school that I didn't want to spend another five years being told what I needed to learn. Nor did I want to work a meaningless, low-paying job; but as an eighteen-year-old, my options for making good money were limited. I gave full-time work a try. After six months of making barely enough money to live on, I was so ready for college.

Eighteen months later, I graduated with an Associate Degree in Electronics and started my career as a Manufacturing Technician. During the interview, I liked the company mantra of, "If it breaks, fix it." Unfortunately, once I took the position, I realized that they didn't actually repair the parts—they simply replaced them. My degree skills were useless. Their mantra only applied to the repair technicians, and there was a waiting list of more than three years for that role.

My job consisted of nothing more than loading parts into the tool, pressing F3 on the keyboard to start the tool, pressing F6 when the tool was done, and finally, moving the parts to the next tool. This engaged me for about ten minutes of every hour. For the other fifty minutes, waiting for the tool to finish, I had nothing to do. No internet access; no cell phone to play games on; no music to listen to; nothing to do but hear the hum of the tools and pray I wouldn't fall asleep on my feet.

I could barely drag myself out of bed for that job. The chance that it would become a long-term career was zero. The good news is, the company was supportive of continuing education, and they paid for me to go back to school and get a degree.

I worked full-time while attending school, and three years later I graduated with a Bachelor of Computer Information

Systems. While I was still in school, I transferred to a position creating computer programs. My enthusiasm for work was rekindled, and I was thirsty for knowledge. I envisioned possibility for a career as a computer programmer.

Almost immediately I hit a major roadblock that would shape how I presented myself to others. My first assignment was to support an application created by another programmer in the department. As I was still learning and needed a fair amount of guidance, I turned to the most logical person for help — the predecessor of my position. Unfortunately, that person was unwilling to help, and all I got was the cold shoulder. No pointers. No guidance. Nothing. Nada. Zilch. "Google it." It was maddening!

And, unlike today, where Google answers all, finding answers online was not easy. Learning came primarily through paperback books and attending in-person classes, neither of which was as efficient as asking your co-worker. I wouldn't last long in a field of programmers who behaved this way. I vowed right then not to follow their example. Instead, I would willingly share my knowledge. I would rather be poor than to have people hate working with me.

In spite of this rocky start to my career, I was determined to not let one bad apple hold me back. I worked my butt off for fourteen hours a day, six to seven days a week, without overtime compensation. It paid off, at first. In my first five years, I earned three promotions and the title of Senior Software Engineer. I was having a blast creating software programs that made other employees' lives easier, but I longed to be in charge. I wanted to decide how we would program the software our customers requested; I wanted to pick what technologies to use; I wanted to select the processes we would follow to deliver our software. But I would need two more promotions beyond Senior Software Engineer before I would be given those responsibilities.

I finally managed to get one of the two promotions, but then my career dove headfirst into a pile of quicksand that I couldn't escape. No matter how hard I worked, the next promotion eluded me. Year after year, my review from management was positive with no critical areas for improvement. I was certain at every review cycle that this would be the year I would get the promotion I so desired. Throughout each year—for ten years—there was zero indication that I wasn't on track for a promotion. Something was amiss, but management wouldn't tell me. I was tempted to look outside the company, but as the sole income earner in my household, I was afraid to leave behind my guaranteed paycheck and great benefits.

The final straw came when several senior leaders suggested that, in order to advance, I should take a temporary assignment with a group that we just partnered with. The suggestion didn't thrill me, as the assignment included no leadership opportunities, and the work felt boring. But I put aside my reservations and accepted it in order to get my promotion.

The new team raved about me to my management and even asked me to extend my stay in their group from six months to twelve months. This was it—I would finally break through the barricades surrounding my promotion! Everything was coming together. I just had to wait a few more months for my yearly review, and promotion would be mine.

Can you guess what happened next? That's right. No promotion! Just another pat on the back for a job well done. If I was doing such a great job, why wasn't I being promoted? I was ready to blow my top!

For more than ten years, I put my all into the job. Something had to change. I couldn't continue to have the promotion carrot dangled in front of my face, just out of reach. Gigantic problem, though: I had nothing that I could show the outside world. All of my work for the company was inward facing. It was the company's intellectual property, and I would be sued if I shared any of it. This made me an unknown in my field. I had no network to turn to and no personal brand. No hiring manager in his right mind would pay me what I was worth. With a résumé void of details, I didn't even merit an interview. I needed to figure out how to brand and market myself without being sued.

After I waddled around for six months trying to figure it out, an unexpected opportunity fell straight into my lap that would change the trajectory of my life. In conversation with a Meetup organizer, I suggested a future topic. The response was, "When would you like to present it?" That wasn't what I had in mind—I was horrible at public speaking! But I was willing to try anything to land a new job. I agreed to present three months later, hoping that would be enough time to develop and practice a good presentation.

Instantly, my fear of getting on stage, making a fool of myself, and being rejected reared its ugly head. *What am I getting myself into?* But I was determined to overcome my public speaking woes. I consumed every article, blog post, and video on public speaking to try to eliminate my fear. I analyzed videos of speakers I admired to reverse engineer how they successfully delivered their talks. I had never spent so much time preparing for a single presentation, ever.

Three months passed quickly. I could only hope that, on the day of the presentation, all of the learning and practice would pay off when I got on stage. I had butterflies in my stomach like never before. Could I really go through with it? I am eternally grateful that I didn't back out.

The talk went over well with the audience, even better than I had hoped.

The next month I received more positive feedback. Two attendees at my talk implemented my content in their office. That was satisfying, and I was hooked! I wanted to get right back on stage.

Later that year, I talked at my first conference, Desert Code Camp, in my hometown. While there, I talked with two speakers who would present at a similar event in Los Angeles the following month. I was unsure whether to accept their invitation to speak. I had never spoken outside of the Phoenix area. Fear and hesitation engulfed me. I would know only two people at the event. I had never driven that far alone. What if no one showed up for my talk? My wonderful, supportive wife encouraged and nudged me (forcefully!) to say yes.

That was the best decision I ever made. The participants, speakers, and organizers were welcoming and supportive, even when I showed up ten minutes late. My Uber driver had tried for nearly forty minutes to maneuver around a number of road closures. Finally, he pulled over and told me the ride was over. I was a mile away from where I needed to be, carrying a heavy backpack in a place I'd never been before. After misinterpreting Google Maps and walking in the wrong direction, I made a U-turn and hauled butt. I had a mile-and-a-half to cover in ten minutes. I prayed I wouldn't be *too* late.

Finally, I walked into the room to see standing room only with almost forty people waiting. I apologized profusely for being late; they graciously said they understood, and they had even warmed up the projector for me. I took a moment to catch my breath, wiped away the sweat, hooked up my laptop, and then I gave my talk. The audience was thoroughly engaged, and I was jazzed to do this again, minus the Uber drive fiasco.

In the next year, I submitted applications to speak to as many places as possible. My employer wasn't willing to pay for any of the travel or even to promote my talks, but they allowed me to use vacation time to go speak. I used three of my four weeks of vacation to speak at twenty-five different events throughout the United States, plus an outstanding trip to speak in Oslo, Norway. I was having the time of my life.

In the past five years alone, I have spoken at more than seventy-five events and have given more than two hundred talks. And I discovered that I love giving all-day workshops where I can dive deeply into a topic. (Who'd have thought someone like me — a shy, introverted, terrible speaker — would love being on stage for eight hours presenting a workshop?) In addition to speaking, I am now an organizer for the DevOpsDays Phoenix conference and the Arizona Give Camp Non-Profit Hackathon. And I am one of only four thousand people worldwide to be recognized by Microsoft as an MVP (Most Valuable Professional).

No longer do I worry about finding another job if I need it. My network has grown from zero to hundreds of people around the world. I have made countless friendships with people whom I would never have met if I weren't on stage speaking.

My experience led me to found Speaker Coaching Specialist, where entrepreneurs, authors, speakers, coaches, and programmers hire me to convert the powerful messages in their head into material they can confidently deliver on stage.

No longer am I the invisible leader, just hoping for an opportunity. I now make my own opportunities, and I love every minute of it. Life has never been better!

I did finally get that promotion, and now I am seen as an expert both within and outside of the company. Public speaking has opened more doors and provided more opportunities than I ever dreamed possible. What doors and opportunities await you?

To take your career to the next level through professional speaking, visit Justin at **www.letyournerdbeheard.com**

Justin James is an Arizona-based, International Public Speaker, award-winning entrepreneur, and founder of Let Your Nerd Be Heard. He works with techies to get them on stage confidently communicating to more than just 1s and 0s and be seen as the go-to expert.

Growing up though, Justin was too shy and fearful of the stage to share his own message. Then at age 37, Justin found himself unfulfilled and stuck in his career. He needed to make a change when an opportunity fell into his lap conquer his public speaking fears and get him on stage sharing his message. In the past, being too shy had always stopped him, but he was determined to conquer his fear. Instantly, Justin realized what he had been missing all these years by keeping his messages inside and he fell in love with the stage.

Justin is passionate about getting you to your end goals faster and specializes in making the complex simple and easy to understand.

Connect with Justin

Web: www.letyournerdbeheard.com

LinkedIn: linkedin.com/in/digitaldrummerj

Facebook:facebook.com/groups/121296064217

Scan this QR Code to view our interview with:

Justin James

https://youtu.be/KQjp6BAw6aI

Chapter 12

Looking into the Eyes of my Father

By Jackie Simmons

Startled, shocked, I held my breath.

In one dizzying instant I was transported away from the professional offices of Veterans' Services and back fifty years...*Daddy?*

...the smell of Old Spice filled the hot car. Even with the top down on the old white Thunderbird, the smell surrounded me as Daddy drove us through our sleepy southern town on the way to a cookout.

Jeanne's sitting shotgun in the front seat next to Daddy, her 16-yr-old self, forgetting to act all grown-up in the excitement of having Daddy home. Millie and Linda are with me in the back seat, all trying to talk at once, eager to catch him up on the excitement of the school year that just ended. A whole year Daddy had missed while on tour. A year that for the four of us was marked by skinned knees, spelling bees, and boyfriends; and lots of arguments with Momma.

A normal year, except Daddy had missed it, again. Daddy had missed most of the last three years. We hadn't really seen him since we waved good-bye from the back of the ship that took the four of us and Momma back to the States, in the middle of my first year of school.

Daddy stayed behind on Okinawa; he was going on tour to someplace called Vietnam and this time we couldn't go with him. This time we were scared, though no one really told me why. I thought it was because we would be on the road over Christmas, driving from California where we got off the ship, all the way across back to Fayetteville, NC where Momma had a teaching job and new schools were waiting for us girls.

Christmas on the highways was marked with fast driving, racing two cowboys in a white mustang on a straight stretch of road that seemed to never end. Pumpkin pie from a roadside diner and somehow Momma found Christmas Stockings made of plastic netting and stuffed with candy and little toys and a note from Santa saying our car was too full, so he'd leave our other gifts for us at our new house.

Made sense to me, and those gifts were the best thing about our new house.

We learned that new schools, mid-year, in small southern towns were no place for "Army Brats." Especially ones whose Daddy was gone, fighting "someplace we don't belong."

Three years of uncertainty, what we now call bullying, and hiding out with my face in a book were all forgotten as we rode through town.

None of that mattered now, Daddy was home! Daddy was home, and we were headed for grilled hotdogs, burgers, and maybe even marshmallows. Daddy was home with his Old Spice and rubbing my face with his scratchy beard. The day was bright, and the car was bubbling over with high-pitched voices, all four of us talking at once until suddenly the brakes slammed and the tires squealed as Daddy hauled to the right, fast as lightening pulling hard on the steering wheel…

We bumped over the curb onto a sidewalk; I was tossed to the floor, my face pressed to the carpet, my sisters on top of me and Daddy using his hands and body to cover and protect us as best he could, not letting us move, barely letting us breathe… and in our ears…the lingering sounds of a firecracker.

It was July 4, 1968. We girls were in North Carolina but Daddy. Daddy was still in Vietnam. We thought he had come home.

We were wrong.

In that instant, on the floorboards of the car with the wind knocked out of my 8-year-old body, I knew the man who just hurled me to the floor wasn't my Daddy.

It couldn't be; my Daddy played cards, and took us fishing, and taught us how to stay safe around fireworks, firearms, typhoons; and in that one instant, on the floor of the car, I was afraid of the soldier that used to be my Daddy.

The summer wore on and the plans of camping for a month by the Neuse River were exciting. Momma had to work, so we got to go with Daddy all by ourselves. Fishing, junk food, soda pop, and card games. It was almost like having Daddy back; except when he lost at cards and lost his temper or drank so much beer that he lost his place in the game.

By the end of the summer, I had gained so much weight that none of my school clothes fit and Momma threw a fit and fussed about the junk food and never questioned why.

After the camping, Daddy was leaving again. Not for war, at least not one they talked about on the nightly news. One night, we sat in the living room in a row on the sofa and learned that while Daddy was overseas fighting to protect our country, Momma and Daddy had been fighting a different kind of war.

Being the daughter of a soldier wasn't common. Living in more than one state, much less more than one country wasn't common…and when Daddy walked away the next morning, with him went any hope of ever being able to fit in, ever again. See, divorce wasn't common either, and when Daddy walked away from our home, in my mind, my Daddy became homeless.

And, deep down, I felt relieved because I didn't trust him not to drive on curbs and toss me to the ground and I felt guilty because I "knew" that he had nowhere else to go.

Daddy stayed away, he sometimes wrote and rarely called. Sometimes we knew where he was, sometimes we didn't. Momma let us know that sometimes he was working and sent money to help pay the bills and sometimes he didn't. When I wrote to him, sometimes I got a reply, and sometimes I didn't.

Three years passed and Millie, Linda, and I walked out onto the tarmac, waved good-bye to Momma and flew to Alabama to spend a summer with Daddy. Jeanne was away at college, and Millie was 16. Millie turned a little pale when Daddy handed her three Military ID Cards for us and said that Millie had commissary privileges, so she could do the shopping while he worked.

On-base housing, we hadn't ever stayed in on-base housing before. I wondered if it was all like this. There were no pictures on the walls, barely any furniture, and just enough dishes for one meal. We could walk around the base, except where we couldn't; and there were soldiers everywhere.

And, I was scared.

I often stayed home with my nose in a book. Daddy's mother, the preacher's wife, came to visit and sensing I was a little lost, asked if I wanted to go home with her to Florida for a while. So, I flew with Grandma Simmons and landed in the most foreign country I'd ever visited.

The Church of God Campground in Wimauma, Florida had signs at the entrance that explained why Daddy didn't live near Grandma. No Smoking. No Drinking. No Swearing.

Little did I know that those rules were just the tip of the iceberg. I didn't know the rules of life on the campground and Grandma commented on everything I did, from how I set the table to what I wore. It seemed to her eyes that almost none of my clothes were acceptable for a young girl to wear anywhere, but especially not on the Campground.

What I did have that Grandma approved of was my one skirt, and in a skirt my chubby thighs were constantly irritated and so was my attitude. When Momma called and asked if I wanted to come home to North Carolina I said yes, and gratefully flew home. At least I thought I was heading home.

I mean, I knew where home was, didn't I? What I didn't know was that my going "home" to Momma's had not been the plan. Daddy had gotten the on-base housing only because the three of us were coming to live with him. Momma had agreed, but no one had told me so when Momma called, I was clueless.

When I flew to Momma's, the deal was off. Daddy's tone on the phone was chilling. Didn't I know that I was supposed to come back to Alabama? Didn't I know that I was supposed to live with him now? Confused, I let Momma take the phone.

I heard Momma say that Millie and Linda had to come "home" now too. That it would be wrong to split us up and it was time to register for school, and I don't remember the rest. I just knew that I was helpless to stop the chain of events.

Millie and Linda were coming home, and Daddy? It seemed that Daddy was going to be homeless, again. And again, I knew it was my fault.

All of this was tucked away in the past when I arrived at the offices of Veterans' Services on the last day of May 2018. I hadn't thought about any of it in a very long time. In fact, over 30 years had passed, and I had long since claimed a sense of safety in the world.

It hadn't been easy.

I'd spent years in counseling and therapy, and I spent a fortune on medication which could get me stable but couldn't cure me. Not willing to risk the re-occurrences of my own traumas, I kept looking for a cure, I shifted into the world of eastern medicine and deep dove into shiatsu–a journey into chi-energy, mindfulness, and meditation. I collected Certifications-the way some people collect vinyl records. I trained with thought-leaders in transformative mediation, human performance, body-mind connections, and entrepreneurship.

I approached the veterans' event knowing I was at the top of my game. I brought copies of my best-selling book for the participants. I knew I would be able to help. I had overcome my fear of soldiers and was coming into Veterans' Services to teach networking skills and elevator pitches to veterans on the verge of, you guessed it, homelessness.

I walked in the door and looked into a pair of slightly vacant, slightly widened blue eyes, the scent of Old Spice filled the air, and suddenly I was looking into the eyes of my father.

Daddy?

"Breathe. Jackie". *"Take a deep breath,"* the mantra ran in my head as years of stress management training came to my rescue. I greeted each Vet and in each pair of eyes I saw my father, and I almost cried.

"Breathe"

I'd done my homework, I knew they needed the "battle drills" of networking. Not the theories of job-seeking but the down and dirty realities of what a network is, how you build one, and why you need one.

They listened, they participated somewhat, and at the end, I knew that for many of them, knowledge and skills were not going to be enough to stop the slide from joblessness, to homelessness.

They weren't struggling to get jobs because of lack of skills. They were struggling to get and keep jobs because of pride, chronic pain, and the mental anguish that haunts many soldiers. They were struggling with the emotional betrayal that comes from serving a country that doesn't seem to know how to serve them back.

In the space of a heartbeat, I saw that the slide from homelessness to helplessness, and from helplessness to hopelessness was so short that it explained the statistic they shared that had staggered me.

As of this writing, we've lost more of our military to suicide than to combat. It's a number too big to contemplate so here's a smaller one.

Today we're losing our military to suicide at the rate of 27 a day. A DAY! That meant that in the time I spent teaching the class, another soldier, possibly somebody's Daddy, couldn't handle the pain and took their own life.

And in that moment, I got it. My Daddy couldn't handle the pain either and he committed suicide too. He just did it on the slow plan. And then I saw all the Daddies and all the Mommies who put on uniforms, and give up their identities as individuals to serve our country and I decided, it's time our country served them back. Since that day in May, I see the eyes of my father in the face of every stranger on the street, and I'm on a mission to end all homelessness, starting with our veterans. I don't know how to solve the whole problem, but I've found a way to address the chronic pain and mental anguish that I know knocks many vets out of the job ring...

My friends thought I was nuts when I told them that I was on a mission to end veteran homelessness and then one of them found a drug-free way to reduce chronic pain and improve stability. A way to improve physical, mental, & emotional stability-without drugs. The products were durable (socks and insoles), drug-free, and new to America.

Finding them was step one.

Then I tested their effectiveness, first with family, then with friends, and finally with the veterans on staff at Veteran Services. The product worked in local testing, not statistics, soldiers. Soldiers, able to walk further, stand straighter, and focus better.

Testing was step two.

If it was your Daddy and there was a way to reduce his pain without drugs, would you want to know about it?

That's what I thought. I knew I liked you. Making the mission self-funding is step three.

Step three: Our mission is to put pain-reducing, high-performance socks on the feet of vets who are struggling to find and keep jobs.

Funding it is where you come in. Not by donating…

By the time you read this, the **www.HelpAWoundedWarrior.com** site will be live.

All we want is for you to share the website, and if you know someone struggling with chronic pain, or wanting to improve their strength and stability, please tell them about the site.

Or better yet, "sock-it-to-them" by buying them a pair. When you buy a pair of socks or insoles for yourself or someone you care about…the sock company helps me sock-it-to-a-vet and…

Everybody Wins.

Our Mission: Help every Vet find their way home, all the way home; physically, mentally, emotionally, and most of all with a place they call home.

www.HelpAWoundedWarrior.com

Scan this QR Code to view our interview with:

Jackie Simmons

https://youtu.be/TForFyQ-mjE

Jackie Simmons

Removing the "Cloak of Invisibility" from her business skyrocketed Jackie Simmons from Secret to Success in 7 Months. BUT it didn't start out that way.

Overwhelm and exhaustion sat on her phone like an unacknowledged, elephant in the room, stopping her from making sales calls, and distracting her so that she couldn't focus and finish projects.

Learning to permanently "tame" the inner saboteurs of overwhelm and exhaustion led to the discovery of hidden rules to a system of success. In her presentations, Jackie shares those rules, and the system that took her first book from concept to published in only 3 weeks and allows her clients to breakthrough what they thought was possible and earn as much in one month as they had the entire year before.

Audiences grin, giggle, & get it, as Jackie guides them into creating their own paths from secret to success.

Chapter 13

Another Level

By Pamela Allen

I dedicate this story to God, who is the author of this chapter in my life. And it is never too late to go to another level.

I am thanking God that I have reached another level of achievement. A professional woman with a master's degree, leaving the city where I was born to accept a position as a corporate trainer, professional coach, and counselor, I dreamed of building a custom house by the lake, and God answered. I dreamed of singing in church with the worship team, and God answered. Talents and abilities that I didn't know I had, were revealed when a country-and-western dance instructor (whom I met by accident) invited me to compete in country-and-western dance. I became a champion.

But I did not want to be alone and sharing the next level of my life with the mate to my soul was a prayer that God had not answered.

Waiting on God is hard. Parents warn us to wait and look both ways before we cross the street, or a car may run over us. "Wait!" they say. "Grab a kitchen towel and put it around your hand before you touch that hot skillet handle, or you may get burned!" I thought I had mastered common sense and that I knew how to wait. But when it came to choosing a mate, I jumped first, without looking, and my blindness led me down a dark, seven-year path of domestic violence, destruction of my business, and death of the only child that I would ever have.

My Plan, Not God's Plan

I did not wait on God to choose my marriage partner, and that was my first step outside of His plan. In my twenties, I accepted the marriage proposal from a young man in church. It seemed logical.

He taught Sunday school and had a college degree. His parents were active in the church and well respected. The church family believed we were a great match. But I was the one who insisted on pre-marital counseling, and he resisted. He told me there was nothing that an older Pastor could tell him about the responsibilities of a husband that he did not already know from his own study of God's word. He finally agreed, reluctantly, to attend each session.

During the last session of pre-marital counseling, the Pastor asked us to discuss our dreams of the future. That's when my fiancé revealed his need to control. My fiancé told the Pastor that, since he would be head of the household, I would trust his decisions for our future. I was informed that I would withdraw from graduate school, so that we could start a family; that I would withdraw from singing in the performing arts chorus; that I would withdraw from the plan to audition for an opera chorus. He would even expect me to cancel my gym membership; and he would build a gym for me at home, because he did not like other men assisting me with my form while lifting free weights. After this declaration, my fiancé smiled, while the Pastor and I sat in a stunned silence.

Soon after that session, the Pastor said that he would support me if I chose not to go forward with the wedding. I did not go forward with the wedding. I listened to sermons from spiritual leaders about God's timing. I believed I needed to do something to make God's plan the reality in my life, but God didn't need my help. He needed my obedience.

One More Step Outside of God's Plan

Unwittingly, I waded away from the safety of God's protection with each plan that I made before receiving His guidance. In my thirties, my plan began with a Christian online dating service. I hoped to connect with a Christian man who wanted to be married and have children according to the expectations of God. My checklist was extensive, because I was specific about who would fit the bill—mentally, physically, and spiritually. Again, I did not ask God to reveal this to me, and I did not wait for His timing.

I was not particular regarding race or ethnicity, since one of the most important characteristics of the mate to my soul was that we share our faith in God as our Father, the Holy Spirit, and His Son, Jesus Christ. After my extensive interview with the Director of the dating agency, she managed my connection personally. She created a match that she believed would result in a marriage made in heaven. He was an older Caucasian male, divorced, with shared custody of pre-teen children, and a business owner with a master's degree. We attended the same church, and he attended every Sunday. I believed my plan would be perfect, but it led me into dark places that I did not expect.

I missed the danger signs.

Missing the Danger Signs

The "match" was an independently wealthy man who chose to work, to manage his own business, and to work out at the gym seven days a week. He ate healthy meals and insisted on family time with his children, despite his divorce. But beneath the façade, he was a functional alcoholic. As I took my life to another level, he took his alcohol consumption to the extreme. He gradually began asking for more help to manage tasks in our daily routine, including household chores, taking care of the kids, even walking the dog. His hands shook, and he was unable to write checks to pay bills. He frequently lost his wallet and his keys.

Drinking a single beer led him to consume an entire case in one sitting. He "needed" the alcohol to relieve his stress after a hard day at work. His memory lapses became more frequent, and his pattern of disappearing early in the morning and late at night became more pronounced. Soon, his body succumbed, his irritability and restlessness increased, and he was agitated with severe mood swings. Some days he was so depressed that he would cancel all of his appointments and stay home from work.

Soon I became aware that he took prescription drugs to "manage" his work anxiety and his back pain from old college sports injuries. He also took medication for insomnia. Because a licensed physician prescribed these drugs, he felt justified in his daily use. I was slowly sucked into the secret, realizing I had missed all the danger signs of functional alcoholism moving into prescription drug abuse. No one would suspect what was happening behind the doors of our upscale home in a neighborhood of fellow professionals just down the street from private clubs and gated communities. The man went to church in the morning after drinking his breakfast and eating prescription drugs. He laughed as he said that his best work was done when he was drunk.

I couldn't believe it was happening to me, and I didn't want anyone to know. Had I not learned the lessons from my own family members who had died of alcoholism? As a child, I had witnessed women in my family beaten, bloody, and bruised. I felt as if a generational curse reached out and grabbed me from the grave when I, too, fell victim to the verbal and physical abuse. I have lost count of the women who became a part of his sexual addiction, including the prayer partners at our church, his female AA sponsor, and the matchmaker at the dating service! I hid my bruises, made excuses to be absent from work, lied about everything being fine when it wasn't. I kept his secret while I bathed and fed him during his moments of major depression and his suicidal declarations.

Shame became my sickness. Why did I stay for seven years? I believe his moments of function kept me tied to the dysfunction. I stood by for his counseling, for rehab after rehab, and for the desperate hope for delivery on his promises to commit to sobriety. I was reminded to believe in restoration and unconditional love, but I lost sight of how love is truly defined by God. I believed that I served a God of a second chance, but I did not consider that He had to choose and that I could not make that choice for Him.

As I drifted further and further from the shores of stable life, I became disconnected from my family and friends and distracted from my business. I lost my house by the lake and a six-figure corporate training contract just before the night that cost one life and nearly cost another.

From Loss Back to Life

One night after a holiday, my fiancé got out of bed late at night to engage in his routine of binge drinking. He raged more intensely than I had ever before witnessed. I was in the very early stage of pregnancy, and whether or not that had anything to do with my decision, I refused to get out of bed, despite the crashing of glass and furniture I heard from the other room. I refused to look into the eyes of drunken rage. The verbal abuse at my back was vicious. And then silence, the shadow of a shotgun, and a "click." Mercifully, the gun did not fire, and he passed out. Terrified and traumatized, I crawled into a corner of the bedroom and prayed.

As I prayed, I felt the sharp physical pains of miscarriage. I cried until the sun rose, my blood soaked the carpet, and our golden retriever licked my tears. When I knew that my unborn child was now gone, I also decided to leave. I now realize that I had the strength to make that decision because I didn't think about it—I had simply prayed and asked for God's plan.

Another Level

Losing my child and nearly losing my own life took me to another level. I returned to my commitment to God's plan and timing, and I walked out of domestic violence into a doctorate. I must admit that I was restored in the non-traditional way. My prayers opened the vision that God intended. I was not worried about how I would do it or where the finances would come from. I took a walk of faith without my human plan as a safety net. Relieved from the distraction, I discovered more of my gifts.

My life continues to be non-traditional, and as a non-traditional online college professor, I facilitate courses with adult working students who have the determination to obtain degrees in higher education. I have a non-traditional approach to coaching and mentoring others who benefit from non-traditional paths to awaken their passion and purpose that takes them to the next level in their lives. I discovered my ability to write and present at a professional level. After I prayed, God sent me a vision, and I am fascinated that the topics are all about the non-traditional approach! God also delivered a non-traditional mentor who helped me make the vision a reality.

I have continued to fulfill my purpose by sharing what I have learned and creating teams to present at conferences across the nation and around the world. My publications appear in peer-reviewed journals, because I trusted that God would reveal to me the plan, the right people, the right place, and the right time. When I commit to a prayer about the plan, God puts me in position to proceed.

"For I know the plans I have for you" declares the Lord. "Plans to prosper you and not to harm you, plans to give you hope, and a future." *Jeremiah Chapter 29 Verse 11 Bible, New International Version*

"We are hard pressed on every side, but not crushed, perplexed but not in despair, persecuted, but not abandoned, struck down, but not destroyed." *2 Corinthians Chapter 4 Verses 8-9 Bible, New International Version*

I discourage focus on regrets for personal or professional plans that created distractions. My plans led me into a desert of my own making for seven years. Despite our intellect and rationale, we can miss the signs leading us to another path that God did not intend. But God knows our value and will not leave us there.

We are human. We get distracted by our own plans instead of waiting to hear from God. We keep secrets that strangle us into silence. We allow the appearance of function to mask deep dysfunctions in the lives of diverse individuals and families. What are you hiding that God doesn't already know?

It is never too late to break the chain of silence, to walk out of your desert, and to obtain another degree in life lessons. In my fifties, I am writing a Christian devotional book; I wrote a Christian contemporary song; I'm starting a business; and I have relocated to another state to start a new life.

Imagine what your life would be like at another level. Imagine taking a non-traditional path to fulfill God's plan and God's purpose in your life. Be open to non-traditional prayers that can lead you to take non-traditional positions of power that bless not only your life but the lives of others in unexpected ways. My victory is not only deliverance from the violence, but commitment to a new vision.

I have never married, and I have no children, but I appreciate value in my non-traditional life. As my life moves to another level and God reveals His plans, I am reminded of my spiritual truth:

I am thanking God that I have reached another level of achievement.

Scan the QR Code below to view our interview with:

Pamela Allen

https://youtu.be/oiYD-9Lt91c

Dr. Pamela Allen had a doctorate degree in Management and Organizational Leadership, facilitates college-level online courses, publishes in peer-reviewed journals, presents at research conferences across the nation and around the world, while managing a woman-owned small business.

But her life has been far from traditional. The normal timelines for a college degree, marriage and children never happened according to the clock of society.

She sings classical music instead of gospel and discovered talent for competing in country and western dance. During the best moment of her life she mastered contracts in corporate training that was moving her towards a dream career and her vision of a house by the lake.

Then a toxic relationship took this professional off her path leading her into seven years of domestic violence, despair and near death.

But a divine intervention allowed her to emerge from domestic violence into a doctorate that created a second chance and positioned her to rise to another level.

Now, her business is called Another LVL, spelled in a non-traditional way. She creates a non-traditional approach to teaching, training, coaching, and even writes about non-traditional paths in life. From her experiences she has learned that, **"For some of us there is a non-traditional path with non-traditional timing, leading to non-traditional purpose that places us in a non-traditional position to fulfill our destiny."**

From her spiritual deliverance she believes that, **"We are hard pressed on every side, but not crushed, perplexed but not in despair, persecuted, but, not abandoned, struck down, but not destroyed."** 2 Corinthians 4: 8-9

Connect with Dr. Pamela Allen

E-Mail: allenppsalm23@gmail.com

Chapter 14

Author of My Life

By Melodee Meyer

I picked up the phone before the end of the first ring.

"Hello?" I asked cautiously, afraid it was the call I was waiting for.

"Hello, ma'am, this is Sergeant Bleeker. We've found your husband and your son."

My heart jumped into my throat. My stomach fell. I was afraid to ask the next question.

"Are they… alive?"

"Yes, ma'am," he answered, "but we need to pick you up and take you to them right away."

"What's wrong? Is the baby okay? Is he hurt?"

The sergeant continued as if he had not heard my questions, "A squad car will be there shortly."

Before I could take a breath, the police were on my doorstep. I walked outside, and without a word, they opened the door to the back seat of their car like I was going to prom. But I wasn't.

I never went to prom. In fact, I had never been on a date before I married the first man who paid attention to me.

I had a lot of theories about why I was unlovable. Was it because I wasn't pretty enough or smart enough or talented enough? Or was it because I was too tall or too fat or too loud or just too much trouble? I couldn't figure out this heartbreaking mystery.

No one else seemed to have that problem. Growing up, my sisters always had boyfriends. Even my parents were madly in love. I used to pretend that I was terribly embarrassed about my parents, but I had a large collection of photos of them kissing at home, at church, and everywhere in between. I so wanted to have that for myself someday.

Then *he* came along. He was good-looking, funny, and bright. Best of all, he thought I was, too. He did have a bit of a temper and was extremely jealous, but to me, that only proved how much he loved me.

When I got pregnant, he was thrilled, and my strong religious upbringing made my decision to get married an easy one.

Within days of our wedding, we moved to a small town in a different state, away from all family and friends, where he wanted to attend Bible college. Little did I know how that decision would change my life forever.

As the police car turned into the parking lot, I recognized my husband's office building. We parked next to several other police cars whose drivers stood in a semi-circle looking skyward. I followed their gaze, and my heart stopped.

On the landing of the second-floor fire escape was my husband with my baby in his arms. *What was going on?*

A policeman with a megaphone called up to him, "Sir, please step back inside." No response. "We need you to come down from there, sir."

I got out of the cruiser and walked toward the building. A female officer pulled me back. "No, don't," she said.

My husband didn't like Bible school. He didn't like studying, and shortly after we arrived in our new town, he quit and took a job as a part-time photographer for the paper. His fiery personality did not mix well there, and he was relieved when they fired him, even though I was nine months' pregnant. We had no money to buy groceries, yet he decided that it was a good time to start his own photography business.

He took over some empty offices on the second floor of an old brick building downtown, and my dad helped with the much-needed renovations.

I liked to have my parents visit. My husband was nicer to me when they were around. He had become more and more aggressive and angry with me with each passing month. *This is my fault.* My pregnancy was wearing me out, and I had little energy to take care of him the way he wanted. *If only I knew how to be a better wife.*

He always felt bad after he hit me. He'd come to me crying and begging for forgiveness. How could I not forgive him? After all, I had said things I shouldn't have said, and that pushed him over the edge.

I thought things would get better once we had the baby, but it only added another level of anxiety and fear for me. I never knew what would set him off, so I tried to keep me and the baby out of his way as much as I could.

I hadn't done a good job of that today. We'd had an argument that started to escalate, so I was grateful when he stormed out of the house, giving me and our sleeping son some reprieve. An hour later, when he marched back into the house, pushed me aside, and walked directly to the baby's room, I panicked.

"What are you doing?" I asked.

He snatched our sleeping son out of the crib and gave me a look that sent a chill up my spine. "Remember, this is your doing," he said, and he stomped out of the house.

"WAAAIIT!" I screamed as I chased him, but he was already in the car and driving away. I called the police, but they explained there was nothing they could do. Apparently, it's not against the law for a father to take his child.

I sat by the phone and waited until, sure enough, he called. He wanted me to know that he was really going to do it this time. He was going to kill himself in front of our son so that he would know what his mother had driven his father to do. "But maybe the baby has to go, too, so he doesn't have to grow up with a mother like you."

I cried. "Please don't! Please…" He hung up.

I called the police again, and due to this new information, they would try to locate him right away.

"Sir, we need you to bring the baby downstairs," the policeman said, his voice strained. "Your wife is here like you asked."

"I'm not coming down. If she wants the baby, that bitch has to come up here to get him."

I pulled away from the cop who had my arm and ran to the ladder. She could not hold me back.

I walked up the fire escape that, on any other day, would have been too scary to navigate. *Is this it? Is he finally going to do what he always threatened he would?*

When I reached the top, I held my breath and reached out for my son. I wrapped my hands around his ribs and pulled him close as I quickly went back down the fire escape. The cop below bellowed something indistinguishable into the megaphone as a distraction.

Without turning back, I was in the cop car again, heading home. But I wouldn't be there for long. The policemen stood over me while I packed a few things and then took me and my son to a women's shelter.

The shelter was a nondescript home in a suburban neighborhood that was surprisingly quiet. A kind girl sat down with me in the kitchen to take my information as my son played with a pile of blocks on the floor. I commented, "I guess we are the only ones here?"

She shook her head. "Actually, we have a full house right now." I looked at her quizzically. "It's just that everyone is at a funeral this afternoon. One of our residents went back to her husband last week. He got mad and slammed their three-year-old into a brick wall."

I felt like I'd been punched in the gut. *What?!*

In that moment I realized the gravity of my situation. That could have been my son. That could have happened to me.

I knew then that things needed to change, and it had to start with me. If I wanted to save my life—if I wanted to save the life of my son—I had to make a change. So, I did.

I stood before a judge and told my story for the first time. I was terrified. But something had shifted inside of me. I was in touch with my worth, perhaps for the first time in my life, and I was ready to take full responsibility for it.

My husband was taken to a facility to get help for what we would find out was a mental illness. I began my new life, not knowing exactly what I would do, but knowing that I could and, that I would.

Being a single mother made me dig deeeeeep. I believed that all things work together for good, and it was time to put my faith into action. I had to learn how to rely on myself, how to reinvent myself, and how to take responsibility so that I could change my life. I had to reimagine what was possible and take the first step to make it happen.

Self-Reliance

I had very little confidence. After all, I had made some bad judgments and some bad decisions, and I wasn't sure if I could trust myself again. But when I remembered how I felt as I stood in that women's shelter, I realized that I had stopped listening to myself and handed that power over to someone else. It was time to reclaim my Self.

To build confidence, I needed to rely on myself.

Confidence is earned, not learned. We earn a little bit of confidence when we stand up after we've been knocked down. We earn a little more when we stand up for ourselves and listen to our inner voice, rather than all the other voices outside of ourselves.

Confidence grows when we realize that we are scared, and we move forward anyway. Confidence grows when we stop blaming somebody else for the condition of our lives, even if that somebody is us.

Reinvention

I've reinvented myself several times. Reinvention is evolution.

By definition, reinvention is the process by which something has changed so much that it looks to be entirely new. When you reinvent yourself, you appear to be a different person, and you are. You are no longer run by your old set of beliefs. You are not only *being* different, you are a different *being*, capable of completely different results.

Reinventing yourself is an inside job.

Do we always have to hit rock bottom to make such a radical change? Simple answer is no. But you do need a strong *why*.

Anthony Robbins teaches that there are two motivating forces: the desire to avoid pain and the desire to gain pleasure. It doesn't matter which of those you choose, but the strongest *whys* have qualities of both. When your *why* is strong, your reinvention is not a goal, but rather a commitment — with no Plan B.

Responsibility

My story doesn't own me, it informs me. It is part of my success education that propels me toward the things that matter most. When I take full responsibility for everything that has happened in my past, I build the confidence to write my future.

Taking responsibility is not the same as accepting blame. Responsibility empowers, while blame enslaves. When you take responsibility, then you can also take the action necessary to change the outcome.

For example, I was not to blame for the abuse that I endured. But when I took responsibility for being in that situation, suddenly I didn't have to be there anymore. My choices opened up, and I was empowered to choose something different.

Reimagine

When working with my private coaching clients, we start with you reimagining all the incredible possibilities available to you.

What do you want? Do you have a compelling why? What kind of work do you want to do? What kind of relationships do you want to have? What kind of difference do you want to make? What kind of body do you want to live in? What kind of lifestyle do you want to live?

It all starts in the imagination.

Did you know you can actually change the chemistry and hormone levels in your body by changing your thoughts? You are a creator. You are the author of your own life. You wrote the story that puts you where you are right now.

Sometimes we feel helpless and inadequate when we hear the success stories of others. We feel so far from where we want to be, but we don't know where to start or what to do next. That's okay. Self-reliance does not mean doing it all on your own. It means you know yourself well enough to know your limitations, and you have the courage to ask for what you need.

I don't regret the pain and the violence I experienced, because it has shaped me into the woman I am today. It has inspired my personal mission to help others find their passion, monetize their expertise and boldly create their ideal lifestyle.

Clarise

A coaching client of mine was at her wits' end. She worked a sixty-hour-a-week job that she enjoyed, but she knew she could not sustain the pace to make the impact that she wanted. Her health was suffering, her relationships were shaky, and she had no time to enjoy her life. She was unfulfilled in her high-powered corporate position and felt stuck in her own success. She knew from a very young age that she wanted to make a big difference in the world, but she was losing hope that she could ever make that happen.

Then she got fired.

Suddenly, the safety rope to which she was tethered disappeared. After a period of disbelief and grief, she realized that things would never change unless she changed. Clarise got the support she needed and worked with me to help guide her through the process that she knew would be challenging but, oh, so necessary. She reimagined the life she wanted, and together we went about the business of reinvention.

With her new vision and a concrete plan in place, she moved into a whole new future for herself as an entrepreneur, making a powerful difference for those she serves. Currently, she is writing a book to build her credibility and her tribe, so she can have an even bigger impact in the world.

What impact has this had on her life? She got engaged, she lost excess weight that she had carried for years, and she now has a business that is built on her values and her mission. She is the author of her own life.

So am I. So are you. What story will you write?

Scan the QR Code below to view our interview with:

Melodee Meyer

https://youtu.be/z3v1-CYtS-M

Melodee Meyer | Speaker Author | Advisor Founder of Kickstarter Club

Creator of the Ultimate Bestseller Formula

Melodee Meyer is a bestselling author, keynote speaker, and personal advisor who teaches entrepreneurs, coaches, and speakers how to kickstart their new business ideas and create the lifestyle of their dreams.

Melodee is the creator of the Ultimate Bestseller Formula that teaches experts how to write, publish, and market a book to build their business without putting their life on hold. She received her master's degree in Spiritual Psychology and is a 6th Degree Black Belt Master, twice inducted into the Karate Union Hall of Fame.

Melodee is the author of several books, including two #1 international bestsellers: *Black Belt Power* and *Clean Food Diet: The 21-Day Clean Eating Guide to Lose Weight, Reduce Inflammation, Boost Energy and Look Better Naked.* Her award-winning programs have taught thousands of folks how to love themselves lean, fit, and healthy so that they can create the life they want, in a body they love, and be the difference they want to see in the world.

Chapter 15

Turning Points are Disguised Blessings

By Mayadari del Sol

"I got the results" the Doctor said, "What is happening is that you are pregnant."

I felt like my whole Dream Castle got knocked down. Back then, I was an artist, the only deliveries I wanted to make were paintings. I had always dreamed of the "Perfect Life," and I used to think that I had the whole world in my hands, beauty, health, financial independence, success from my painting, and all the material things I wanted. How could I know this was going to become a turning point in my life?

I don't know if it was selfishness, fear of the unknown, or both but it was hard for me to cope with the news. I knew many things were about to change and I didn't want that, but also deep inside me I knew there was an inner fear that I couldn't consciously recognize, and I didn't want to confront it.

I was 33 years old when Diego, the art dealer, came into my life. He didn't live in the States; he was from El Salvador, he would travel back and forth dealing art from different artists. That's how I got to meet him. We didn't have a formal relationship; we had been dating for some time when I found out I was pregnant.

"Now what?" I called him with the unexpected news, and to my surprise, he said, "Well, let's get married". I was shocked.

Somehow, his proposal didn't make sense to me.

I liked him but not enough to marry him. I wasn't sure if he was going to be the right man for me, and I didn't know him very well to make such a decision. What I was expecting was a different kind of support, more of the emotional and affectionate. When I told him my feelings, he thought I was being selfish because I shouldn't think of me anymore but the baby and what he needed, a family. I don't know if it was me or what? but still, I didn't feel comfortable with his proposal. I felt like he was pushing me into that, and I didn't want to accept it under pressure because of the circumstances.

So, I proposed back to him to stay around, to support us, and if things worked out between us after the baby was born I would consider his proposal. He didn't agree and decided to disappear from the scene. That was the end of the relationship. I didn't get to see him again. Somehow, his attitude made me realize I wasn't wrong about my decision related to him, but at the same time something inside me had been awakened, a feeling of abandonment.

I couldn't recognize the feeling of abandonment back then. All I knew was that I had become what many people called a single parent from the beginning, and of course, I felt lonely.

Most of my family lived overseas, in Colombia, which left me more isolated. My pregnancy had emotional up and downs, more downs than ups. Yet, I decided that I had to continue doing the outdoor Art Shows to make money until the last moment because I didn't know how things would be after the baby was born.

I tried to stay strong, but between the change of hormones and the roller coaster of emotions and thoughts, I found myself powerless, crying many times. There was one thing I remembered doing every day. I would ask the Divine Spirit, "Why things happened like this? I don't understand. Please bring answers. Don't leave me alone. My soul hurts".

Angelo was born December 11, 2005 at 8 a.m., around Christmas time, the quietest and darkest Christmas ever. To begin with, I got the postpartum blues which took me down in depression. I acted strong when it was needed but deep inside I was broken. I felt very vulnerable. I couldn't be present beyond my emotions. Not even the sweetest beauty of my son was enough to lift my heart up.

Since January through April is the best season to sell art in Florida, I decided to go back to the 2-day outdoor shows right away. What a season! I have countless stories of traveling every weekend, struggling with a just born baby in a car loaded with paintings, the tent, diapers, bottles, and all sorts of baby items for different needs, all by myself. It was crazy! I went through all kind of emotions. Each one would make me stronger but not in a positive way. I created a core that seemed strong, but it was based in anger. I was angry.

Where was this feeling coming from? I couldn't recognize it, but I could recognize who I was angry with, the masculine. I felt anger towards men. In my belief, "They hurt, abandon, abuse and betray".

My perspectives kept taking me down the road until the somatization got to my body. Suddenly, I had symptoms of fatigue, tiredness and exhaustion. I started taking long naps often. The more I slept, the sleepier I was, until I fell in a deep and dark hole. I didn't want to think or feel anymore, the only thing I wanted to do was to sleep. I was depressed.

By then, Angelo was more than one year old, and he was very active. I remember his face standing by the bed calling me, "Mommy, mommy get up" for which I replied, "Angelito, give me 5 more minutes", that would become hours.

For security, I decided to ask my mom to come and take him to Colombia. I was aware something was wrong in my body, but I didn't have health insurance. Also, by 2006 the economy in the United States went down, and I was struggling to make money from the Art Shows. Just as I said at the beginning, my whole Dream Castle fell, my health, my finances, and my life in general.

Then, when things couldn't be any more dysfunctional in my life, I got a call. The turning point that brought me here, was trying to take somewhere else. When I got to the bottom of the hole, in my sleep, I heard a voice saying, "Maya, wake up! It is time". I was ready to heal.

To begin with, I needed help, I decided to go to Colombia to get checked, and I found out that I had hypoglycemia, which was the reason of feeling so sleepy and tired, which was my escape not to think or feel anything from the world. If I analyze hypoglycemia, hypo means low, and glycemia has to do with the sugar in the blood, and I was feeling a lack of love or sweetness in my life, especially from myself.

While I was in Bogota, I got to meet someone that was very connected to what I was ready to receive. This is where my journey of healing began.

I understood that to heal my body I needed to heal my mind, my spirit, and my soul. So, I traveled to Chile to a tribe called Condor Blanco, where I had an experience of change. I needed to forgive, let go, rediscover, and empower myself.

I took a course for certification of conscious awakening for women to heal and reconnect with the feminine, and one in leadership.

First, I was an apprentice, then a practitioner and later a facilitator.

This was my beginning teaching consciousness to others. After this, all the doors of the holistic field that were open, I visited. Anything that would bring wellness to me.

I navigated different healing and balance techniques. In the synchronicity of the universe, I had the honor to meet my shaman teacher, Heidi, who taught me energy healing for years. Then, I learned and facilitated Qigong and Taichi. I also offered Guided Meditation and Thought Consciousness for several years. Later, I became a Florida Massage Therapist, a Health Coach, a Nutritional Coach, and a Life Coach.

By 2013, I felt on track. My body was healthy, I was cultivating my energy, my mind was tuned up, and I had found a side of me as a healer that gave me peace and satisfaction. Still, the journey of my own healing was only half-way done. I needed to get back to the road to heal the other half of me, my soul. Thus, only the wisdom of the universe aligns new experiences for us to confront what we need to see, to heal.

By January 29th of that year, on my birthday, I received a special present. For the celebration, some friends came to my house and one of them brought a musician friend, named Diego.

"What of coincidence!", the same name as the father of my son. Love was knocking at the door, and I opened it, literally. I am not sure if I got enchanted by the music or if it was the universe orchestrating this encounter to take me into the new learning adventure.

So, I got tricked, and I fell for it. There I was, getting into a relationship with a man that was not involved in my path, neither in my lifestyle, but played music beautifully. In my mind, I thought "Maybe all we need in a relationship is love, a good connection, and music".

We made some agreements for the relationship to work out. Still, when it came to communication we were in different states of mind. I worked on understanding and accepting his perspectives, even though I couldn't agree on many of them. Somehow, I felt this was a good opportunity to learn acceptance, and to let go of controlling what you cannot change in people and in situations.

Four months later, suddenly, I started feeling physically tired, with lack of energy, and unmotivated to do my practices. One morning, in one of my daily routines at the gym, while in class, I felt I was about to faint. I stopped what I was doing, went to the restroom and sat there for a while until I recovered. I thought I had a sugar unbalance. What came to my mind was, "Could this be hypoglycemia again"?

So, I went home and decided to take a week off to recover.

The following week, I decided to go back to the same class. To my surprise, about the same time of the work out, I started feeling the same sensation. At that point, I recognized something was wrong. I needed to get checked. So, again the same game plan, since I didn't have health insurance, I decided to fly to Colombia to see a doctor.

I finally heard my name being called in the waiting room at the Doctor's office. By then, I was having the symptoms of a man in a cartoon when he sees the sexy girl for the first time, my eyes and heart were popping out of my body. I could listen to the lub-dub lub-dub of my heart going very fast. Effectively, the Doctor told me I was having a dysfunction with the thyroid called hyperthyroidism.

The symptoms included intense heart palpitations, shaky hands, and fatigue. Besides, the metabolism in my body sped up so I was losing a lot of weight and hair, and my eyes started to pop out like a frog. The doctor didn't give me hope at all. He said this was going to be a permanent condition. He told me to take a medicine that is common to treat overactive thyroid twice a day, for one year, to begin the treatment. His plan was to take me from hyper to hypoglycemia until it got balanced.

I replied saying, "That doesn't make sense to me. Why don't you just give me medicine to take it to the balance point? By then, my thyroid will be messed up, won't be doing its job and will be dependent on the medicine".

Then, he gave me this saying we use in Colombia "But this is the solution here and in Capernaum", which is a place in Galilee where Jesus cured people. I said, "No, I don't think so". He gave me the prescription and I left.

I came home very disappointed and sad. My family suggested I should buy the medicine just in case. But in my consciousness, I didn't believe it was my body.

"How could it be my body when I eat healthy, and I stay strong by working out and practicing wellness?". If I had decided to believe I had hyperthyroidism, I would probably be taking medicine for it until this day.

I am glad I listened to my inner voice that kept telling me, "It isn't your body, look deeper". So, I decided to go for alternative medicine while I could find the cause of my imbalance. I stayed in this journey for a few months in Colombia.

Meanwhile, Diego was already leaving the relationship because he couldn't understand why I wouldn't take the medicine, come home and live a "normal life" with this condition as part of it. I didn't feel supported by him. He broke up with me over the phone, took his things and left. I felt sadness, but mostly a deep feeling of "abandonment" again.

I came back to the States and went through the whole emotional recovery of feeling abandoned again. I couldn't practice or facilitate classes because I wasn't energetically or physically up to it. I felt dishonest to be teaching balance when I was feeling completely off balance in my life. I had a moment of confusion, frustration and sadness. I remained like that for another five months.

Even though it was hard for me to meditate, I didn't stop asking for answers every day, "Why am I feeling sadness? after all, my boyfriend and I weren't having the connection or communication in the level I wanted for a relationship. What is it that I need to understand, accept or let go of? What is the missing piece?"

On December 31st of that year, the miracle happened. That night I wasn't in the mood to go out to do anything, so I decided to stay home. It was just my seven years old son, Angelo, my dog Gypsy and me. We gathered in a cozy carpet in the middle of the living room to celebrate and to be thankful for a new year. By midnight, they were both sleeping. I was getting messages from many people, until I got one from Diego, "Happy New Year, can we talk?", which I was open to.

He came over around 1 a.m. We sat and talked about different things until we got to the subject of our relationship. What I could understand about what he expected from me in the relationship gave me a different perspective. The problem was that we didn't establish a clear agreement about us in the beginning of the relationship, about each of us as individuals and our own purposes.

He pretty much expected me to play the wife role, which I happily played while we were together, but he didn't consider me as the empowered woman who follows her individual dreams to fulfill her life purpose. The thing was that I was clear about my path and he knew it. I noticed his disappointment. That was the end of the conversation.

What surprised me was that after he left I felt emotionless. I sat on a pillow in my meditation corner to rewind what had just happened. Then, I had a blissful moment. I felt a relief and I entered in a state of peace and comprehension.

I heard the inner voice in my head asking, "Was that what you really wanted? I said, "Hell no, not at all", and we laughed together. "So, if is not about him, what can it be?", the voice asked. "It is about me", I replied. I could clearly see that what hurt was the feeling of abandonment, not the person, and that I didn't like experiencing that feeling and I didn't know why.

The next day, January 1st, 2014, I woke up like myself again, very motivated and happy, ready for a new beginning. About two weeks later, very close to my birthday, one morning I felt so great that I decided to go back to the gym for a cycling class. I wasn't supposed to do any cardio because of the heart palpitations, I had stopped working out for almost 8 months already. It was crazy, but I thought "The worse than can happen is that if I feel the palpitations, I'll leave the class".

I was happily greeting my friends that I hadn't seen in a long time, the music was on, I got on the bike and I started cycling. I kept the resistance low. To my surprise, I made it through the whole class and I felt amazing.

When I came out of the gym I looked up to the heaven and said, "I am well, all is well".

By then, I had health insurance. So, I decided to get checked. I didn't tell the Doctor about my condition. I simply asked her to get me tested for everything, including T3 and T4. A couple of weeks went by before I received the call from my Doctor's office, "Your results are ready". I had a mixture of emotions and thoughts until the Doctor said, "All your levels of everything are well balanced.

Congratulations!"

Outside in my car, I cried. Many lessons had been learned. But what I was more thankful for was that I realized I wasn't ready for a relationship. I had something beyond my understanding to review, and to heal, related to the masculine in my life, and this Warrior wasn't going to give up until finding the truth.

When you need something, and you ask for it, the universe always brings answers.

First, I started studying the wounds of childhood and how they affect you as an adult. Of course, I could recognize my wound of abandonment right away. Then, I met a couple of psychologists who were doing Family Constellations, a therapy to heal the genealogical tree and the ancestors. I put my studies together to acknowledge how they can be related.

It happens that the memories from childhood get imprinted in a cellular level, so they are harder to recognize. The perception of the child creates wounds that stay dormant throughout our lives and as adults we attract experiences that awaken the wound when we haven't healed it, and we don't notice it.

I hadn't seen things from this angle before, but I started reviewing my life to find that when I was 8 months old, my mom put me in a baby carriage while she was talking to my uncle in the kitchen. The carriage had wheels and I started rocking it until I rolled down the stairs. When my father came home and noticed the bump on my head, he got mad at mom, took his things and left.

Two things happened here. First, I energetically registered the abandonment as that, "my father doesn't love me, he abandoned me", that eventually got transferred to the masculine in my life. Secondly, I felt guilty for the separation of mom and dad, like the incident in the carriage was my fault, and the cause of their separation.

What was this imprint doing? Throughout my life and since I was 13, most of my boyfriends would leave me. I was being loyal to the abandonment without noticing it. If I had a stable relationship, I couldn't believe he would love me enough to stay, so I would abandon him before he abandoned me. That way, I didn't have to feel the wound of abandonment again, that was my unconscious pattern.

But, how did this dysfunctionality originate?

I started studying the genealogical tree and how the stories of our ancestors still affect the descendants of generations. I found out that my Great Grandmother Rosa was very young when she married a General, who died, and she was left with two kids (abandonment). Then, she got married for a second time, with Juan, and they had 3 children. He died (abandonment again).

One of these children was my Grandmother, Minda. My grandmother named my mother Rosa. My mother married Julio, my father, who left us after my incident with the carriage (abandonment). Her second relationship was with Juan, they had 2 more kids, and she abandoned him.

I am not blind to what I see, and this isn't a coincidence. The abandonment was an ancestral memory to heal in my family, and this is just one piece of the whole puzzle.

Can you see other details? Like Great Grandma Rosa married a Juan just like my mom Rosa who married a Julio, that starts with the two first letters of Ju, and then a Juan. She was following an invisible pattern. She carried the energy to heal from Great Grandma so strongly that even the names of her men were similar, or the same as hers.

On my father's side there were also stories of abandonment. My Grandma Lola left my Grandpa Lalo (abandonment), because he went through a financial loss that he couldn't recover from. So, my father also was carrying the wound of abandonment.

I compare the dynamic of the genealogical tree with a sport called Sprint Relay. Relays are races in which teams of runners take turns running around the track, passing a stick, called Baton to their next team-mate, until the last runner gets to the finish line.

The same thing happens with our ancestors. We are a team; great grandma passed the stick to grandma, who passed it to your mother, and she passed it to you.

We are racing to heal something, and we don't even know what it is. So, we are passing the baton from generation to generation to see who finally finds out what needs to be healed.

The finish line ends when the last team-mate consciously understands what was needed to heal, and does it, to liberate the whole team from it.

We choose parents with the same wounds we come to heal. We accept the experiences to come before even incarnating in the body. That is part of the journey as a human. I see and understand why my son Angelo already has felt the wound of abandonment from his father, just as it happened to me. We both chose to heal it but also had it dormant in our genetic code.

I realized this not long ago. I finally got to see where it came from, and I liberated it. I showed it to my son, Angelo, with comprehension and love, so he can see it too.

Angelo is 12 years old now, and I feel blessed I found this truth to share with him, so it will save him part of his journey.

What it is beautiful from finding the truth, and liberating it, is that it gives you peace and confidence to walk freely in life. And, that as much as you heal the ancestors you help the whole tree heal. The descendants and the ascendants are liberated.

There is so much to heal in the ancestral tree, not only the one from your family, but from humanity. The origins come from the beginnings of creation and we have gone through a lot of pain in history. That's why I decided to become certified in Family Constellations, back to the Transgenerational healing needs as well. Even before we are born, all this legacy to heal is passed onto us, and that is why we live experiences without comprehending the origin of them.

Most people think that what happens in their life is a matter of luck or coincidence, I don't agree. Most of the dysfunctions in our health, finances, love, relationships, family, and the accomplishment of your dreams is related to the genealogical tree. As a Life Coach, the first session I do is the analysis of the Genealogical Tree, so we can reprogram from the unconscious memories. Then we can address the mind easily, creating a plan and feeling confident about it.

To close this story, I finally understood that what was causing me pain was not the person who left, but the awakening of the wound dormant inside of me. I also understood that healing the wounds of the soul, or the memories of the ancestors, does not happen in the mind. They need a different reprogramming, in a cellular and an energetic level.

That is how Healing Alchemy Formula was created, 3 steps to recognize what limits us. To transform, not only self-limiting perspectives, but unconscious memories through a creative experience that can reprogram us in a cellular, mental and energetic level. To empower us with confidence, and the freedom to attain any dream, goal or purpose. So, we can all expand consciously in the world.

Today I feel gratitude for those men in my life. They were only mirrors for me to see what I needed to heal. They abandoned themselves when they left, just like I felt myself when I thought I was being abandoned. Beyond that, today I understand that no one leaves us, that the abandonment doesn't exist as we are all one inseparable unity, and that it only exists in the mind of the perceiver.

Life presents challenging journeys we don't like, but the universe knows when we are ready for them. Saying yes to these Turning Points is saying YES to receive the infinite blessings of healing for all. For yourself, for your genealogical tree, and for the oneness of humanity.

Scan the QR Code below to view our interview with:

Mayadari del Sol

https://youtu.be/o3v9jq3BvRY

MAYADARI del SOL is a Transformational Coach and the Founder of Healing Alchemy Formula/La Jornada del Heroe (in Spanish), one of the most supportive, online and live programs for the transformation of self-limiting beliefs and unconscious memories for the fulfillment of the Self. For more than 12 years, Maya has been devoted to searching and applying tools that can help people recognize and transform their own limitations, as well as ways to keep body, mind, and spirit in balance.

After going through a turning point in her life that impacted not only her physical body but her soul, she took on a journey for healing. For that, she understood that to heal her body, she also needed to heal her mind, the unconscious memories that came from childhood, and the ancestral memories that were inherited which can be the roots of most of the limitations and fears in people's lives.

To begin her healing, Maya decided to cultivate body, mind, and spirit. So, she became an apprentice, then a practitioner and later a facilitator and teacher of practices like Meditation,

Tai Chi, Qigong, Energy Healing, and Aromatherapy. Furthermore, she also became a Licensed Florida Massage Therapist, a Health Coach, and a Life Coach.

The second step in the journey of her healing was the soul. Maya studied the dynamics of the Genealogical Tree and the ancestors, as well as the wounds of childhood to be able to liberate unconscious memories through recognition, acceptance, forgiveness and gratitude.

Today, she is getting certified in family constellations, and is the author of a soon to be released book called *12 Keys to Unlock Your Hidden Reality* with observations that can help people realize their own hidden limitations.

Before being in the holistic and wellness field, Maya was dedicated to art. She was a professional dancer and traveled around the world with a Colombian company. Then, she moved to the U.S. where she became a painter. She made art exhibitions and outdoor Art Shows, where she won many awards and accomplished great satisfaction. Today, she considers herself an Art Therapist, since she uses a creative process that involves arts to heal, transforming and reprogramming the unconscious and limiting perspectives throughout it.

Maya is the mother of an amazing boy, Angelo, who happened to come to this world to be part of her turning point journey. For that, and for their love and connection, she feels infinite gratitude.

One of the things that Maya enjoys the most, besides helping people, is nature and playing by ear when traveling, to allow the universe to surprise her.

She has built a conscious community group in Kissimmee/

Orlando, Florida, called "Empowerment for Inspirational Warriors" to practice wellness and to participate in her Healing Alchemy program, which helps people get transformed and empowered to move confidently towards the fulfillment of their dreams and goals.

To connect with Maya, follow these links. Websites:

www.HealingAlchemyFormula.com in English

www.LaJornadaDelHeroe.com in Spanish

Facebook, Instagram & LinkedIn: Mayadari del Sol
YouTube: Mayadari del Sol

Email: **limitless@mayadaridelsol.com**

Phone number: 1 321 9005680 U.S.

Chapter 16

It's About Time—and Intuition

By Matilda Jarmy

It had to stop. I couldn't stand it anymore. Enough with jumping through everyone else's hoops! It was time for me to run things my own way. I did the next logical thing. I quit. Walked out and moved on.

I felt free and terrified!

Immigrant Work Ethic

My parents were immigrants, fleeing Hungary after Russian Communists had taken control of the country. I am eternally grateful for their sacrifices, so our family would have better, safer lives with endless opportunities. They taught me the importance of family and keeping your word, and they demonstrated a powerful work ethic to provide for loved ones.

The tradition of my generation and my family was to go to college, get a job, work our way up the ladder until we make it, and then retire. Don't question the status quo. There's no time for wishes and dreams when you're in survival mode. You have responsibilities, you shoulder them, and you keep going. My parents didn't have the luxury of time to delve into their dreams.

They had escaped tyranny, and they took jobs as necessary to create a decent life and provide for their family. Surviving meant putting dreams on hold.

That philosophy seeped into my subconscious. Responsibility first. Dreams later—if ever.

My dad always put his team first. He protected his people. I grew up thinking that all managers act that way. I was about to learn some hard lessons.

For most of my early career, I unquestioningly followed that path: get the degrees, go to work, do your best, eyes on the prize, get that promotion. Never once did I pause to reflect or to ask myself, "What do I want?" "Do I enjoy what I do?" "Does this work light me up?" Those questions didn't see the light of day for many years. I kept them deeply buried, hidden from view. But they lurked under the surface, nonetheless. I was not content. Something felt off. I tried to subdue my vague discontentment by starting and dropping one side business after another.

The Corporate Ride

I moved to New York City in my twenties and started a trajectory that would change my life in ways I couldn't imagine.

Looking back on my career, I now recognize and acknowledge all the times when I wanted to break out of the corporate constraints and run things my way. My intuition said to serve clients my way, to treat them the way I wanted to be treated. My instinct was to take care of my team the way I saw my dad take care of his people. I wanted to do things right, to demonstrate loyalty, and to receive loyalty in return.

But that rarely manifested for me in the corporate world, and when it did, it didn't last long. My values were at odds with the corporate culture: profit for profit's sake, watch the bottom line. While that is prudent and necessary, it lacked the human element. Staff wasn't highly valued or made to feel like we're all in this together. I preferred to focus on the client. I believed, "The customer comes first," "The customer is always right," and "There's no I in Team." My early career was a great training ground for learning how to multi-task, plan and run projects, and in general, keep projects moving forward. I loved the challenge and was fully committed to the organization. I happily worked sixteen to eighteen hours daily, got fantastic results and I earned promotions in rapid succession.

My Game Changers

In early 2001, my son Miko was born, and it totally changed my life. I went from total career focus, working sixteen-and eighteen-hour days, to seeking balance of family and work. I still worked full time, but I needed to rebalance my life. I had waited a long time to start a family. Now that my son was here, he was my primary focus. I asked to work four days in the office and half a day from home per week. Work/life balance was a hot emerging topic at the turn of the millennium. Our company even had an onsite backup childcare facility. On the surface, granting this request should have been a no-brainer. I could maintain my career while carving out much-needed family bonding time.

Not so fast.

Though they granted my schedule request, they told me point-blank that I would never again be considered for promotion, because I wasn't taking my career seriously. *What?* Wow!

The Game Changer

I was told to choose between my child and my career. That was a stunning development and lot to process. Twelve months prior, my manager had assigned me to a mission-critical project—a project she said no one else on her staff could pull off. I assembled the required team and completed the project. A year later, I'm attempting to process their view of working mothers. There was no question, no hesitation. I happily altered my career trajectory for my child.

A few years later, we moved to Charleston, South Carolina, and I made the first of several attempts to run my own business. My previous corporate experiences led me to entrepreneurship, even though it was a bumpy, tangled path. During my ride on this entrepreneurial carousel, my son Marcello was born. My pregnancy with Marcello was high risk. I spent ten weeks in the hospital and another three weeks with him in the second level nursery. I couldn't even think of work, let alone be productive. Marcello came through with flying colors. My time with him was invaluable and life-changing, for both of us. When he came home, he needed extensive care for several months, which only confirmed my decision that corporate life wasn't for me.

But as necessity would have it, one more corporate gig was on my horizon. The need for medical insurance and a steady income forced my hand. For the next few years, I worked long hours as an IT project manager, I raised two small children, I trained in martial arts, and I watched my marriage unravel in slow motion.

Countless days I had no clue how I would get through the day, let alone tackle my growing to-do lists which spilled onto scraps of paper and the backs of torn envelopes.

I wanted to spend time with my sons, and I also wanted a career. The juggling act required to pull that off was burning me out, but there was no way I would give up either one. I had to figure this out and create a balanced life. I needed a holistic approach, but I had no roadmap. My friends were in the same boat. We tried our best, attempted to juggle everything, but came up short exhausted as devoted, conscientious, working moms.

Conventional wisdom guides us to start where we are, so I took little steps to get organized. I drew on the skills I'd learned managing projects for Fortune 100 companies. I put my own twist on them and slowly created order amidst all the chaos. It wasn't perfect, but little by little, it got easier. Still, I felt vaguely dissatisfied within the constraints of corporate life.

It would be easy to set the blame at the feet of corporate culture and say, "I was just a cog in the machine." But that is non-productive and completely misses the point.

Tuning In

The nuanced truth is that I wasn't in conversation with myself. I wasn't tuning in to my intuition about what to do and who to be.

I am immensely grateful for all the time and training those organizations and corporations invested in me. I did my best to give value in return. But in retrospect, it was never a fit, and that created friction: they wanted me to conform, and I wanted to stay true to myself. Although I can see that clearly now, that lack of alignment wasn't obvious to me then. What slowly manifested for me was a vague sense of dissatisfaction. My intuition quietly tried to get my attention.

Intuition told me to engage in work that aligned with my vision for myself, my life, and the clients I serve. That's what nagged at me. My lack of alignment between my purpose and my work had been building up for years. My intuition had been gently nudging me to make a change, and I wasn't listening. Finally, the nagging became loud and insistent.

I had been on a successful, but highly stressful path that compromised my health, threw me off balance, and took time away from my kids. I tried to separate work from family, but that juggling act burned me out. That's when I decided it all had to stop. The hours, the stress, the juggling and the way I engaged with work. It was time to look at career fulfillment and motherhood in a new way.

Even this roundabout detour served me well, however. I developed a valuable set of skills. By working through the daily and weekly challenges, always prioritizing my kids first, I developed a framework of prioritizing without regrets. Driven by my desire to actively pursue career and motherhood, I learned how to *master* my time, not merely manage it.

I realized then that I had been misjudging my corporate experiences. There was never anything wrong with the way I approached my work, or interacted with clients, or carried out my responsibilities. I was just in the wrong place, trying to stay true to myself while checking all the boxes and doing what was expected. Once I understood the futility of that, I was able to stop treading water and move forward.

As I decompressed from a high-stress career and tuned in to my intuition, the vision for my life became clear. My solution didn't come from separating the various aspects of my life, and it didn't come from work/life balance. Fully integrating family and business was the key to make it all work for me: happy kids, happy mom, a thriving business, and time for friends, family, activities, and adventures. My intuitive clarity allowed me to fine tune my time mastery skills in a way that NOW allows me to have it all, without feeling overwhelmed.

Now I live an exciting, integrated life. I no longer have to choose between work and family. It's all integrated, exactly the way I always wanted it to be. Is it perfect? No. It's a very functional work in progress.

My days flow with ease, and I have time for everything that's important to me. I enjoy a flexible schedule that allows me ample time for my children, family and friends. I work with amazing clients and teach them how to master their time and focus on their most important priorities.

Living an exciting, integrated life is within your reach. Here are some essential steps for your journey:

1. **Maintain a sense of humor**, especially during the tough times. It lightens the atmosphere and calms your environment.

2. **Stay clear with yourself** on your wants, needs, dreams, and goals. Regularly check in with yourself to be sure you're on the path that is true for you. Correct course as necessary.

3. **Listen to your intuition.** It's your internal guidance system that keeps re-directing you towards your best self. Intuition is quiet and fleeting, like a wisp of smoke. Your intuition is never fear based. It never leaves you in a gut-wrenching state of panic. Panic happens when your ego tries to get the upper hand. Tune into the difference between ego and intuition. It's the best investment you'll ever make.

4. **Take assessments** that reveal facets of your personality and interaction style. The more you know about yourself, the more effective you will be in all areas of your life. Self-awareness is the truest form of power.

5. **Invest in yourself.** Personal development is a crucial component of this journey. Invest in mindset training, personal healing, business development. Let your path of personal development become a lifelong habit.

6. **Hire a mentor** to help you up-level your life. Evaluate where you need the support — personally, in business, with your health. A mentor will guide you through the growing pains of expansion and shave years off your learning curve.

It's definitely true that experiences shape us. I wouldn't be who I am and where I am today without my varied life experiences.

When those experiences are combined with time mastery and intuition, you can create a rich, multi-layered life with a clear vision for your future. Are you ready to create your amazing, integrated life?

Scan the QR Code below to view our interview with:

Matilda Jarmy

https://youtu.be/Xhx2Udg6SqM

Matilda Jarmy is the founder of Optimize Your Time, specializing in training and mentoring business owners in the essential skills of time mastery, business systems and marketing automation.

She is the creator of "Ultimate Time Mastery", an integrated life approach to time management, designed for small business owners who are juggling business ownership with parenthood. Business owners learn to integrate the various threads of their lives and analyze opportunities with a proprietary "Prioritize without Regrets" system.

Matilda had a 25+ year career in consulting and IT project management for Fortune 100 companies, managing projects in New York, Europe and Asia.

She uses her business acumen and her unique blends of skills to help small business owners create freedom and flexibility in their business, so they can make more money and spend more time with their families.

Website: **www.optimizeyourtime.com**

LinkedIn: https://www.linkedin.com/in/matilda-jarmy/

Instagram: @matildajarmy

Twitter: @matildajarmy

Chapter 17

"All In"

By Marilyn Sutherland

2003. It's Friday late afternoon and I'm driving to the airport to fly home to Dallas. It's raining buckets, and I have virtually no visibility. I'm going 15-30 mph in a 50-mph zone. I dial my husband, Chuck, but nothing happens – I have no cell signal. When I finally get a signal, he doesn't answer. I'm out here doing all this for him and he hasn't called me all day. I'm upset and scared.

Chuck, a real estate broker/developer, and I have been married for almost 4 years. He needs pictures of a property for a client but has client meetings today. I said I would fly out and take the pictures to support him since I had a flexible schedule. My plan was to fly up (4 hours with crummy connections), rent a car, drive 90 minutes and take pictures of the building and property, drive back to the airport, grab the last flight out, get home before midnight, and sleep in my own bed. That schedule gets me home in time to attend a training course we're both doing on Saturday morning. Now I'm regretting coming, and worse, I'm starting to feel resentful. If he really cared for me, he would answer the darn phone, or check in on me. He's ungrateful and now I'm angry.

My anger builds while I drive, and I start dividing up the furniture. I start thinking through the arrangements for our separation. We each get one of the sofas, I take the leather chairs, he takes the upholstered ones. As the miles pass, I go through each piece of furniture figuring out who gets what, so we can both furnish apartments. Next, I divide up the art, and on-and-on I go. Should I stay in Dallas or return to Washington, DC, where I have more business connections? In an emergency, I know I won't be homeless. I can move in with my dad as a last resort.

When I finally get to the airport, my flight is delayed, then canceled, due to weather. I book a flight out the next morning. I'll be 90 minutes late for the all-day training course we're both taking that starts at 10 am. I check into a hotel (thankfully I got a room), schedule a wakeup call, get a toothbrush from the front desk, and go to bed.

I don't usually remember my dreams but that night I'm dreaming about dividing up the furniture. I wake up ready to divorce him. I check my phone and listen to the message Chuck left the night before. He apologizes for not being able to reach me and thanks me for making the trip. He says he loves me and can't wait to see me. I am dreading seeing him!

My flight lands and I grab a taxi to go right to the training. When I walk in the room, he turns toward me and his face lights up. He's saved me a seat next to him. Not wanting to cause a scene, I sit next to him, then keep my eyes forward, pretending to focus on the class while steeping in righteous resentment.

On the break, we go outside and take a walk around the building, so we can talk in private. I start to cry. "Do you know how scared I was driving in a torrential rainstorm? I tried to call you several times. My phone wouldn't work. Whenever I had a cell signal, you didn't answer! I was frustrated and felt abandoned. Why didn't you call me back?"

He did call me, but his call didn't go through either! He was at a friend's house for dinner with no cell signal. (Remember this is 2003.) He got my messages when he got home, returned my call, and left his message. He had not been able to reach me, and he was concerned about me since I sounded upset in my messages.

As we walked together that Saturday morning, I told him I had already divided the furniture and art and was so mad at him for not being there for me. I'll always remember the horrified look on his face. He was shocked that I was actually thinking of leaving him.

He stopped walking and turned toward me. He wrapped his arms around me and hugged me. Then he looked at me and told me that I was *the one* and he didn't want to lose me. He thought we had something special and that if we put each other first, we would not just make our relationship work, but make it stronger and better than ever.

In that moment, I realized that he <u>really</u> did love me. When I was blaming him, I didn't think about what it was like for him with me. Of course, he was worried about me when he heard my messages. I was blaming him and building a case against him and my story wasn't what really happened.

FINDING LOVE

I married Chuck at age 49. It was my first marriage; his third marriage. Before Chuck, I never wanted to get married, as almost everyone I knew who was married didn't seem to be <u>really</u> happy, at least not by my standards. I did want a long-term monogamous relationship yet was afraid of committing to the wrong man. Has that ever happened to you? Did you ever want a relationship with a deeper connection but were afraid to give your heart because you didn't trust it would turn out for you?

Chuck and I actually knew each other for 10 years before we started dating. We lived in different cities. I lived in the Washington, DC area. Chuck lived in Wichita, Kansas. We had seen each other every year at an annual conference that was hosted by RESULTS, a non-profit working on hunger and poverty issues. I thought he was smart, articulate, and a nice guy. I knew he had five kids and assumed he was married. He wasn't on my dating radar.

The 11th year, I was writing a paper on RESULTS for my graduate school program. I asked if I could interview him and he agreed. When he called me to give comments on the interview transcript I had sent, we connected on a personal level. I learned he had just separated from his second wife. I had a rule to not date men who were recently divorced, much less separated, but there was no harm in talking so we did -every night for two to three hours that first month.

We had our first date in person a month after that initial call. After eight months of nightly conversations (while I was working full-time and in graduate school full-time), I moved to Dallas where three of his children lived. We married four months later. (You can read my whole story in the book The Game Changer: Inspirational Stories, Volume 2 on Amazon. com.)

I was totally at home with Chuck. I could be myself with no pretense. I trusted him. He respected me, my career and my intelligence and wasn't threatened by my success. Chuck was smart, well-read, and I loved talking to him and sharing ideas. He was fun and made me laugh.

Until I started dating Chuck, I had prided myself on being an "independent single woman." Once we married, I had to unlearn nearly every relationship skill I had as an independent single woman and learn to put Chuck and the kids (ages 15-24) first. Everything in my life was new – being a wife and step-mom, learning my way around Dallas, working for a new company, making joint decisions with Chuck, and just having people in my space all the time. On top of that, my mom died a week after our wedding! I was grieving her death. That first year was both the happiest and saddest year of my life.

We were busy with work, the kids, the house – you know, life! Then, BOOM! A year after our wedding and my mom's death, my immune system crashed. At first, I thought I had the flu, but I could not shake it. I was sleeping 20 hours a day and groggy for the other four hours. I was diagnosed with fibromyalgia. Barely functioning, I couldn't work in the fast-paced consulting business. After several months, I was laid off from my job. Tired and depressed, I had lost the familiar, active, exciting, and busy lifestyle I knew.

DON'T LET DISAPPOINTMENTS BECOME BARRIERS TO GIVING AND RECEIVING LOVE

Several months after my diagnosis, with a radical change in my diet, I started to have more energy. Chuck and I began being trained to lead transformational programs which was fun to share. I didn't have the stamina that I had before my crash and so, after our training, he'd go out for drinks and late-night dinner with our friends and I went home to sleep. I wanted him to have fun, but I expected him to want to spend time with me. Instead, I felt abandoned. It took another year for me to get back to a "normal" life.

Now I know that expectations are a source of disappointment when the expectations are unexpressed, unrealistic and not accepted by the other person. When I realized that I had never clearly and calmly shared my feelings and asked for what I needed and wanted, it was unrealistic to expect him to read my mind. Mind-reading is not a communication skill!

HONORING MY VOWS

Our wedding vows are "Partnership, Joy, Love and Magic." When we first began talking on the phone, we had conversations about what we wanted in a friendship with each other. I had no expectation for our future. We came up with "partnership" and "joy" as what we wanted in any friendship -friends, work colleagues, and family. When we wrote our vows just before we were married, we added "Love and Magic." Those four words included everything I wanted to be for him and wanted from him. When we spoke these vows at our wedding, we each committed to generating them every day (regardless of how we felt, or if our spouse "deserved" our efforts today.)

After I got sick, I had pulled away and put some distance between us. I no longer felt like the center of his universe. I was waiting for magic to show up instead of creating it. I honestly thought we were doing well until that drive in the rain when, suddenly, I felt totally disconnected.

Back to our walk around the building. That's when I realized that I was not living any of my vows. I was <u>trying</u> to be a good partner by taking this trip on behalf of him; yet when it didn't work out, I blamed him. Partnership, joy, love and magic were missing!

I saw that I was always waiting for him to betray me in some way, not by cheating, but by disappointing me. This pattern came from the past and got overlaid onto Chuck and our marriage. He was the first man I ever totally trusted, and that trust had been damaged when I got sick. I had never thought about this before, but I didn't want to marry before Chuck because I didn't fully trust any of the men I dated.

During the first four years, when something happened, I would imagine that–instead of working it out with Chuck -I could go live with my dad. By the way, I didn't realize that the solution of 'moving in with dad' was a very convenient back door that prevented me from going "all-in" with our partnership and marriage.

Standing outside that building that Saturday, I committed to him again that I would honor our wedding vows. It was time for me to be responsible for who I was in our marriage. This was my first "game-changing" moment.

CLOSE THE BACK DOOR

Dad lived in Pittsburgh, Pa. After mom died, dad bought a cozy two-bedroom condo a few miles from the house where I grew up. That second bedroom was actually a 10x10 den, already filled with furniture. Not one single piece of furniture I claimed when I was dividing everything up between Chuck and I on that ride in the rain would have fit in that tiny room. I knew that it wouldn't work for me to live in dad's apartment for more than a few weeks but, when

I was upset, it helped me feel like I wasn't trapped (which is the point of a back door).

My second game-changing moment was a surprise. It happened 18 months later when my dad died. I realized that I'd lost the security of having that impossibly impractical back-door bedroom. There was this moment of choice. I could find another back door and go back on my promise to honor my vows, or I could commit 100%.

When I saw the truth of that, and the impact on me, and on my marriage of this perpetual back-door option, I chose being married to Chuck. I promised to keep my vows. I chose to be a real partner, all-in, no back door.

What happened when I did that?

COMMITMENT & FORGIVENESS

I didn't just close the back door. It was no longer an option. After waiting almost 50 years to commit to love with an amazing man, I gave up the right to be however I wanted to be without considering the consequences. Trust is something that happens in the every day moments, hundreds of times a day.

To have an amazing relationship, I had to elevate myself to be an amazing partner. How I was with him no longer depended on him and what he said or did. How I was with him was about me–my thoughts and beliefs, my emotions, what I said and did–and whether I was going to honor my vows or not.

Wayne Dyer said: "When you squeeze an orange, you'll always get orange juice to come out. What comes out is what's inside. The same logic applies to you: when someone squeezes you, puts pressure on you, or says something unflattering or critical, and out of you comes anger, hatred, bitterness, tension, depression, or anxiety, that is what's inside. If love and joy are what you want to give and receive, change your life by changing what's inside."

In the beginning, when Chuck did anything I didn't like– such as leaving dishes on the counter instead of loading them in the dishwasher or not responding to me every time I spoke – I sometimes resented him. Funny thing is, I did those same things, too. I wanted forgiveness from Chuck when I did these things, yet in the past, I reserved the right to be resentful when he did them.

You probably heard about how Nelson Mandela survived 27 years in prison in South Africa, yet when he was released from prison, he was grateful and empowered. If Mandela could forgive his government and prison guards for torturing him, then it was time for me to forgive Chuck for anything I didn't like because whatever got "squeezed out of me" was about me, not him.

BE GRATEFUL

When I let go of expectations of perfection and appreciate how he really is my partner in so many ways, I feel so happy and blessed. When I'm upset, I now think about whether it will be important in a few days, much less a few years, and then I usually can let it go and stand in gratitude for his love and support. When it seems important, I ask to have a conversation and share how I feel, acknowledging my reaction is not his fault. Whatever emotions came out were inside me! If I have a request, I ask him. (NOTE: This does not apply if you are in a relationship with someone who is mentally, physically or emotionally abusive and/or you have any fear for your safety.)

Neuroscience now proves that what we think, feel, say and do forms neural pathways – the more we do something, the stronger the pathway and, at some point, these actions become automatic habits. Instead of spending time unconsciously practicing and reinforcing the pathways for complaining and criticizing, I focus on what I do have and then, I'm grateful. When I tell Chuck (or anyone else in my life) how I appreciate him, it brings us closer.

In what ways can you authentically acknowledge your partner or someone important to you right now? I invite you to think of something and then tell them.

ASK NOT TELL

After committing 100% and being grateful for all Chuck did for me, the next step for me was to make powerful requests. He simply couldn't please me if I didn't ask for what I wanted. I've learned the hard way that blaming, expecting, hinting, and nagging don't work.

Neither does withholding asking for what I need (like when I withheld from him how I felt abandoned and hurt when I was sick).

Most of us have never learned that there are three components in making a powerful request. Clearly state:

1. What do I want (no demands or subtle hints) in a calm voice.
2. When I want it.
3. What are the clear criteria for the listener to complete the request satisfactorily.

Here is an example of a simple request: "Are you willing to stop at the store on your way home and get a bag of frozen blueberries?"

To make clearer the difference between a request and a demand, just imagine I'm saying to you with a frustrated or insistent tone – "You better stop at the store on your way home and get a bag of frozen blueberries!" If this demand impacts you negatively at all when you read this, then you can be sure it impacts others when you speak to them with anything but respect.

The listener has four ways of responding: accept the request (which means are promising to fulfill my request), decline (whether they give a reason or not), postpone answering or counter-offer, which is to propose another set of actions instead of what I requested.

Sometimes it's hard to accept a "no" or "not now." When I accept that answer, I am showing respect. When he makes a request of me, I don't say "yes" to every request either. In the end, an honest "no" is better than an empty promise to avoid confrontation.

Expecting that my partner, or anyone else, will do everything I request (or read my mind) is unreasonable and setting myself up for disappointment.

When either of us do not honor our promise to the other, we acknowledge that. If we can't accept the request, we often suggest other ways to resolve the concern. In a committed love relationship, mutual forgiveness, kindness, grace and compromise help us navigate through the breakdowns that are a part of life.

Trust is created when I honor my promises and damaged when I don't.

EFFECTIVE COMMUNICATION WITH MY PARTNER (& EVERYONE ELSE)

Communicating with love isn't just the words I use. How I

act, my tone of voice, my facial expressions, gestures, and other nonverbal communication are often more important than just the words.

Everything I do has the potential to bring me closer to Chuck or drive a wedge between us.

By being fully invested in my relationship, what I think, feel, say and do reflects my commitment to him. I have stopped asking "What has he done for me?" and started asking "What can I do for him?" and, "What does he need?" For example, if he runs out of something and doesn't replace it, when I'm running errands, I'll get it for him. If he's getting on a business call at noon, I'll anticipate his needs and offer to bring him food before the call, in case he didn't eat anything.

When I honor my commitment with love, my relationship is magical. When I'm feeling like I'm doing more than my share, I feel and act selfish and resentful.

Now, I am usually able to forgive and let go of disappointments and upsets with Chuck. The definition of "forgive" in most dictionaries is to stop being angry or blaming. Neither of us ever did anything intentionally to harm the other and I realized over the years that when I'm hurt, frustrated or insulted, that is *me* reacting. It is not something happening with my partner. When Chuck says something, hurt or anger can squeeze out <u>or</u> partnership, joy, love and magic. Forgiveness allows me to let go of the anger and blame which got triggered. When I forgive Chuck, we're both free from the negative emotions.

Knowing Chuck has my back and has no intention to hurt me, I'm learning to be grateful and appreciative of all he does and of who he is. I want him to know he matters. When I am grateful, he is loving. When I revert to criticism, there is an instant shift in Chuck's mood and openness.

No one, from two-year-old children on up, wants to be told what to do. If nagging worked, the people we nag would happily do what we wanted the way we wanted it done. When I keep our communication open and clean up the upsets as they occur, the foundation of our communication is love and respect.

I've learned so much about myself as I continue to practice healthy relationship skills such as respect, kindness, making powerful requests, and honoring my vows. It's my commitment to share what I've learned from my journey to help other women navigate their relationships. I'm proud of what Chuck and I have created since that day when we walked around the parking lot. Instead of dividing our furniture, we have united inside our commitment to each other, living our vows as the foundation for our marriage. And I bring the same skills to all my relationships – family, friends, colleagues, and clients.

I don't know what your relationship situation is. I do know that we all have the possibility of being better communicators, and newly creating our love relationships and/or our life if we commit to living from love.

My clients have breakthroughs in their communication, confidence, and compassion for themselves and others in their life. I would love to connect with you and see how I could help you have the breakthrough your heart wants in communication, love and life.

When you look at your life, where are you not "all-in"?

Imagine the partnership, joy, love and magic or whatever _you_ want, when you commit to being "all-in." If someone like me, who was afraid to be vulnerable and let love in, could create a great (not perfect) relationship, then so can you!

Scan the QR Code below to view our interview with:

Marilyn Sutherland

https://youtu.be/luTU3F8TbHw

Marilyn Sutherland has spent her life transforming the lives of over 1000 individuals through coaching and consulting. By combining her business acumen and passion to empower people, Marilyn became an author and life coach who helps her clients shift into practicing the essential skills to have powerful, sustaining relationships at home and work.

She is the creator of two transformative programs: "Effective Communication: Deeper Connection" course, and "Your Journey to Lasting Love (YJLL) Program." Through private, couple and group coaching, her programs progressively nudge participants out of behavioral patterns sabotaging their chances at deeper, more satisfying love and work relationships.

Prior to coaching full-time, Marilyn had a 17-year career managing internal and external relationships at IBM. After obtaining a master's degree in Organizational Development, she worked for Accenture as a change management and communication consultant. Throughout her professional journey, she also had a consulting business that coached leaders on managing change; communicating effectively; leading teams; and designing organizations with cultures that support the company's vision.

As a lifelong learner, she is a graduate of Presence-Based Leadership Coach Training that incorporates a broad range of disciplines to have people practice and embody their learning to gain mastery.

Marilyn loves to travel and has been to almost 30 countries. As an activist for the end of poverty, she traveled to Bangladesh, Honduras and Guatemala to see microcredit programs that provided small loans for the poorest women. She wants to visit South Africa to see family; Paris to show her husband the view of the city from the Eifel Tower; and the beach to finish writing her book highlighting what she learned about love from interviewing 100 people on their journey of love from childhood to adulthood.

If you would like to know more about how Marilyn could empower you in your relationships, please contact her at **www.YourJourneyToLastingLove.com** and view her articles on **YourTango.com**

Connect with Marilyn

Web **https://YourJourneyToLastingLove.com**

Products & Services:
https://YourJourneyToLastingLove.com/Coaching-and-Courses/

https://www.facebook.com/marilyn.k.sutherland.1

https://www.linkedin.com/in/marilynkodishsutherland/

Your Tango Relationship Expert Profile

www.yourtango.com/experts/marilyn-sutherland

Chapter 18

You Can Only Save Yourself: A Lesson in Resiliency

By Stephanie Duffey

Late one evening, as I walked down the hallway to my bedroom, my daughter Jane suddenly appears, screaming insults at me. "I want to hit you," she shouts, as her anger escalates into a rage. After yelling at me for 20 minutes, she falls to the floor in an exhausted heap, sobbing deeply and feeling remorseful for her behavior. As I stare at her, I think, "She desperately wanted to live with us and be part of our family, so why was she behaving like this? What did I do to deserve this? What was happening to my life?"

Feeling like I was just hit between the eyes, I dropped to the floor and hugged Jane. She was tired and confused, not even aware of what just happened. As she was coming back to the present, I was still shocked with the intensity of her latest outburst. I knew that she would be in a deep sleep in 30 minutes and then I could have time to absorb the effects of what just happened.

The Decision That Changed My Life

Three years prior to this night, I made a decision that altered the course of my life forever. It seemed like a simple decision at the time, but it would have huge consequences. My journey with Jane would immerse me in a deeper understanding of the human spirit and lead to the most intense emotional roller coaster ride of my life. If only I had known...

While working for a non-profit society, my path crossed with Jane and her mother. Eleven-year-old Jane was living with her mom and younger brother in a small apartment. My supervisor asked me to facilitate an intervention so that there could be peace within the family throughout the weekend. Jane's mom had been struggling to parent Jane for some time and things were getting out of control.

Even though I had good skills around conflict resolution, I could not create a miracle. It quickly became very apparent that, for many reasons, Jane's mother could no longer care for Jane.

Very late on this Friday afternoon, we continued to come up empty handed, searching for a temporary home for Jane. Nothing seemed to be available. It was getting late; everyone was getting tired. I asked for permission to bring Jane home with me for the weekend with the plan that we would resume our search on Monday.

The weekend went well. My husband liked Jane and she seemed to fit right in. My husband's teenage children from his first marriage were not with us that weekend, so it was just the three of us. After some discussion, my husband and I decided we wanted Jane to be part of our family. We believed we could provide her with the stability and safety that she required as well as a sense of family.

Jane was a sweet, quiet, and perceptive girl. For the first few months, life revolved around creating a routine and getting Jane settled into her new community. Jane adapted well and was happy with her new environment and basked in the attention shown to her. We even proudly showed off updated family portraits of our new family.

The Cracks Start

Soon enough the bi-monthly visits with my husband's teenagers became more stressful with each visit. Although Jane appreciated all the attention of being an only child the majority of the time, she struggled with sharing us when the other two came for their weekend visits. Jane was deeply angry – an anger that was well hidden, at least at first. My husband and I were not prepared for what came next.

Summer was upon us and my husband's kids were with us for a month and half. When conflict arose with the kids, my husband and I differed greatly on our parenting styles. He acted more like a friend to the children, whereas I was stricter. He was the "good cop"; I was the "bad cop."

The stress within our family was now obvious. Jane was outwardly aggressive toward her siblings and they did not know what to do. As a parent, I felt helpless and fearful that I could not figure it out. I began to question if we had done the right thing of bringing Jane into our family. I knew that my step kids did not want to spend time with us because of Jane's behaviors and the stress it was causing everyone. Jane seemed to be in control of the family and I didn't know how to dethrone her.

One day my stepdaughter slammed out of the house, saying she needed to cool off after an argument with Jane. "I am sick of my sister's stupid comments and I can't take it anymore," she said. This day was a wake-up call for me. I shared my concerns about Jane's effect on the kids with my husband and the damage this was doing to them. My husband was taken aback and said, "You're not patient enough and the kids need to learn to accept Jane." My thoughts were, "He's putting Jane's unhealthy needs ahead of his own kids. Really, his kids need to learn about acceptance?" I was at a loss.

Now I was beginning to doubt myself and my parenting ability. "I don't have kids of my own so what do I know? Am I being too strict and expecting perfection?" Life was spinning out of control.

After thinking everything over, the next morning I told my husband that I had made a call so that Jane could be placed elsewhere. The way I saw it, Jane was a 12-year-old who could control herself if she chose; she knew the rules. Jane was using me as a monthly verbal punching bag and not willing to accept my step-kids. I was exhausted and no longer willing to continue to put myself nor his kids in emotional harm. This situation was way too much for me and I didn't know how else to make it stop. My husband did not like my decision that Jane was to be placed elsewhere.

A Brief Respite

Jane was quickly placed with another family. We let her know that we loved her, however her behaviors were unacceptable and the cause of her being placed elsewhere. She understood, as best as she could, and was remorseful for the way things turned out. I was still regretful that I couldn't make this work, yet grateful that the craziness had stopped.

Jane started therapy to address her behaviors and I also sought services for myself. I believed I was not a good enough parent, felt guilty that I was not more resilient and a terrible person to have Jane removed from our house. "I should have been more patient", I told myself. "If only I had better coping abilities, greater knowledge and understanding, or experience raising my own children, maybe I could have parented Jane more effectively and things would have turned out differently."

With time and some counseling, Jane slowly returned to live with us again. This time we were more committed to making family life work because we had all done some healing and learned some new skills.

Jane Returns

Apparently, things were not as they seemed. Fourteen-year old Jane was back with us for one month before the school suspended her because of her behavior. I was excited to take a leave of absence from my job to home school Jane. She was a few grades behind her classmates, however, with perseverance, we would get her caught up, or so I thought.

I wanted her to complete her schooling and beat all odds stacked against her. I was committed to taking away Jane's childhood pain and to start her on a path of feeling safe, secure, and happy.

Jane and I would go shopping regularly as she was quickly growing and needed new clothes. She was a great looking girl, had cute hairstyles and was dressed in the latest fashions. I began to wonder why I was putting all this effort into her appearance. As a result of my own introspection, I began to question if I was proud of *her* or proud of *myself* for her appearance. Was I attempting to feel good about myself by boosting her self-esteem? Why was showering her with the latest fashion items so important to me? Was I making up for her pain and suffering as a child or was I healing my own inner child through her? Who was I actually healing?

Home schooling didn't last long nor did Jane's stay with us. Jane's verbal outbursts towards me became more frequent and meaner. Something would set her off and she would go into a rage, and, of course, I would always be the target. My self-esteem took a huge hit. "Why couldn't I parent a 14-year-old girl? My skills are not working." I would ask myself, "What is wrong with me? Why am I getting so stressed out? Am I going to quit again as her parent and walk away? Have I done the best of my ability?" I need to think about the damage I would cause her by abandoning her, yet again. "Am I even worthy enough to be a step-mom to my husband's kids every second weekend and on holidays? Am I that hopeless? I totally suck at being a parent."

One late evening, Jane came out of her bedroom and stood in the hallway hurdling hurtful comments to me and threatening to hit me. I braced myself for another go around, clinging to my self-control. She accepted my rule that she could roar at me for 20 minutes, and then had to stop. Even though she wanted to smash walls, she listened to me when I directed her to the rec room downstairs where the punching bag was set up.

When I could detach myself from what was happening, her monthly rages fascinated me. Her voice and demeanor changed as she screamed hurtful comments. I knew that I needed to attend to her for about 20 minutes before she crumbled onto the floor in an exhausted pile, not remembering earlier events. I told myself over and over, "It is not personal. I am just her outlet as she expresses her deep pain and anger. I can take it. I am the adult. This too shall pass. I can suck it up. We'll be okay. I deserve to take a tongue lashing since I abandoned her and caused her more pain. I'm no different than the other people in her life."

Home life quickly changed again. Jane began spending time with a bad crowd; she was not home for days on end. When she did briefly show up to get some things, she did not look good and would make snide remarks. Although I was saddened to see where her choices were taking her, I was also happy to have a reprieve from her personal attacks.

Cracks in My Marriage

It was during this time that my husband and I separated. Although we did our best to make our marriage work, we struggled throughout our time together because of our differences. Instead of growing together, we grew apart.

With Jane gone more often than at home, I was appreciative of this time to deal with the pain of our dissolving marriage. Even though I knew it was best for my husband and I to part ways, I was surprised that our separation triggered my own childhood abandonment and rejection issues. I realized I was re-parenting myself through Jane. I was giving to Jane what I never received as a child.

A month after my husband moved out, Jane came back home for a few days. Her first days back typically consisted of sleeping for the first two days. Once Jane caught up on her sleep, I broke the news that her dad moved out. She was devastated and blamed herself. I explained that our separation was inevitable, and my ex-husband and I would remain friends.

Shortly after our separation, Jane began a pattern of dividing her time between my ex-husband's home and mine. She was now 16, and still deeply embedded in her behaviors and unruly crowd. I was exhausted and didn't have the strength to continue my unhealthy patterns with Jane. I just wanted peace, quiet, and respect.

The decision whether Jane would continue to live with me became clear when she stole my car key and gave my car to "some guy" to pay off a debt. After this devastating blow, I decided Jane could no longer live with me again. I could not continue to feel unsafe in my home and have my things disappear. Life with Jane had drained me to my core and I knew I couldn't save her.

Within a few months I moved away from our community and found a new therapist. During my therapy I grieved the loss of a failed marriage and Jane. As Jane continued with her self-destructive patterns of drug use and promiscuity, I blamed myself: "Where did I go wrong? Why didn't I see this coming? How could I have been so naïve? I was a terrible wife and parent."

I hit my own rock bottom. I wasn't sure I had the strength or energy to even get back up. I had the ability to only deal with what was immediately in front of me. The future seemed so overwhelming, so bleak, and I was emotionally exhausted and depleted. I was not sure that I wanted to continue living. Life was hard and painful. I gave up on the happy endings that come out of fairy tales. They were meant for others, not me.

Once Jane left my home for the final time and I moved away, she became pregnant and gave birth to her son. Jane was able to raise her son for the first two years before surrendering him to his dad. Jane realized that she did not have the parenting capacity to parent full time. The father continues to care for their child during the week and Jane is with her son on weekends.

I am so proud to report that Jane is now in a healthy and strong relationship with the father of her second baby. She has more visits with her older son and, hopefully will be reunited with him full time in the near future.

Lessons Learned

Although I never believed I would feel this way, I am now grateful for what Jane taught me. I often refer to my experiences with her. Jane taught me that I am a strong person. I am resilient and able to draw on my inner strength. I survived a very difficult time in my life. I came back.

The biggest gift Jane gave me was to learn to honor our own journey. We are on our own unique personal journey. It is not for me to express my opinion or cast judgment of what is right or wrong for another person. It is up to me to honor what that person believes is right for her/him. Our role is to support one another by holding space and listening while setting healthy boundaries within the relationship. We all have the answers within ourselves.

Sometimes we need a listening ear to mirror back to us what we already know.

After a ten-year hiatus, Jane and I have reconnected and have a healthy relationship. Despite her self-destructive behaviors, Jane's resiliency let her recover and heal to become a healthy person. She is happy and successful, on her own terms, and able to reflect on her teenage years and realize, now that she is a parent, what it was like for me to be her mother.

As for me, I am happy with who I am and am so grateful for my journey to get here. Life is amazing, and I am so blessed to be here.

Stephanie Duffey is a Canadian born Entrepreneur and Transformational Facilitator. Although Stephanie has always enjoyed taking personal development courses, it was the crumbling of her marriage that catapulted her into a deeper dive of herself and human behavior. As a result, she found her deeper purpose and is passionate to support others along their journey.

Stephanie Duffey is self-employed as a personal well-being coach, embracing the body, mind, soul connection.

Her mission is to empower and support people to find their voice, speak their truth and stand in their power. Her strength is to inspire others to see their own greatness and potential, so they can feel on purpose and start living the life of their dreams.

When Stephanie is not focused on her business, you'll usually find her hiking nearby trails, walking along the river, reading, or getting together with friends.

Connect with Stephanie Web: stephanieduffey.com

Instagram: stephaniedufffeycoach

Facebook: stephanieduffeycoaching

Linkedin: stephanie duffey coaching and consulting

Scan the QR Code below to view our interview with:

https://youtu.be/yF8zZceDJRk

Chapter 19

His Voice – His Limp His Smile

by Shauna Marie MacDonald

My father called and insisted on coming over. He'd been away on vacation for several weeks and hadn't met my new baby. I decided to make this a pleasant visit. I'd shift the footing in our uneasy relationship. Full of hope, I thought a second grandchild might crack the armor my father wore as protection against external affection. Growing up, Dad's expressions of love were sporadic and often laced with uncertainty. I'd fallen into his habit of strained avoidance when we were together; maybe today would be one of gently adjusting our relationship. I hoped that the innocence of my new baby would be a natural place to begin healing his careful heart.

My three-year-old daughter, Jaclyn, was playing in the yard when dad arrived. He walked passed her without looking in her direction. I found that strange. When I saw his face, I could tell he was distracted, he seemed distraught, as well as in physical pain from a car crash he'd been in years ago. He'd lost his leg in the accident, but more than that, he seemed to have lost sight of his self-worth.

When I was growing up Dad had been quick with a smile, but he wasn't overly affectionate. As a child, I employed all manner of tricks and talents to gain snippets of his approval. He delighted in my spunky personality and my innate ability to win first place ribbons and trophies in track & field. I accepted these sporadic declarations of pride as expressions of love. Interestingly, since the accident, he'd become more openly loving. To my surprise he was learning to express himself. He found it especially easy to show love to Jaclyn and his tenderness toward her made up for the lack of attention I felt growing up. Now he was about meet Andrea, his second grandchild, better than any first-place ribbon or trophy with my name on it. She was my creation.

Andrea lay sleeping in the bassinet beside the table as my father sat and recounted his trip. He'd gone to the United States and western Canada to visit family and friends. Full of pride, I lifted Andrea's tiny sleeping body to my chest, inhaling her sweet fragrance as I kissed the crown of her head. I was filled with love and joy as I turned my new baby toward my father, so looking forward to this moment, above all.

He refused to take her. A bolt of rejection pierced my heart. He reasoned that she was sleeping, and he took a sip of his coffee. Words failed me as I tried to make sense of his actions. I settled back in my chair, the baby in my arms and with confused silence I listened to more of his adventures. While he was talking about his visits with the others, I became aware of a single thought: he was avoiding visiting with me.

The baby woke and after feeding and changing her, I held her in my outstretched arms, ready for Dad to meet and cuddle her. For the second time he refused, saying he was worried his coffee was too hot, he didn't want to burn her. It came to me that he hadn't even looked at her since he arrived. Why was this? My chest ached.

Pressing her tiny body to my heart, I worried that she could sense my sorrow. How could he resist holding this precious innocent child?

While he continued to drink his coffee, my confusion deepened. I slumped in my chair as the familiar anguish from my childhood of never enough love or affection sliced through me. Listening to all the wonderful visits he had… I lost patience. I wanted to scream: pay attention to my baby! I wanted him to pay attention to me *through* my baby. It felt like I wasn't enough, we weren't enough…the hurt that I'd known as a young girl returned. Feeling rejected and abandoned again, I hardened to him. He sensed it was time to leave.

Awkwardly, he turned his chair and body away from me and raised himself up. His limp was more pronounced as he made his way to the front door. I was relieved he was going, speechless under the sting of his dismissal. I followed closely, a cold stare fixed on his back.

He made his way toward his car hesitantly. I called to my three-year-old to come and hug Grandpa goodbye. He shook his head and said, "No-No, it's ok, I'll see her another time." In that instant my Irish temper flared, "DAD, let your granddaughter hug you." He stopped short allowing her to approach… she wrapped her tiny arms around his waist. His back tensed. I couldn't believe what I was witnessing. A grandfather unable to receive affection from his own granddaughter? What was missing in him that made it impossible to gaze into the eyes of my child, smile at her, make her feel special and loved? It pierced the core of my soul. He was rejecting my daughters and he was rejecting me, as a daughter and a mother...a double blow.

My daughter released her hug and skipped to my side. This wasn't the grandfather of the past few years. There was a disconnect in his reaction to her. It felt like he was detaching from her, from us and this behavior of his felt laced with internal pain. As he walked away, all I could see was a broken man. A blanket of pity smothered my bitterness.

With his limited mobility, it took a while to position himself behind the steering wheel. He turned to look at me through the open window, a profound sadness washing over him. He looked deeply into my eyes for the first time that afternoon and whispered, "I'm sorry." Blinking back tears, I nodded, acknowledging his apology. He smiled ever so slightly. I knew it was all he could give. There was always tomorrow, we could try again tomorrow.

With a sleeping baby nestled in one arm, I scooped up my eldest to the familiar position on my hip. I turned from my father, convincing myself that our next visit would be better. With each step, the space between us expanded. I never looked back, but what I heard were two distinct sounds – the slow mechanical rotation of tires pulling away from the curb and three hushed words from my daughter, "Bye-bye Grandpa," the softness of her voice lost in the morning breeze.

Days later, my brother called. He asked if I was sitting down and my heart just knew.

My father took his own life. My father meticulously planned how his life would end. He orchestrated one last visit with everyone, a final farewell.

To my knowledge, the last person to see Dad alive was me. The last arms around him were his granddaughter. The last eyes he looked into were filled with hurt, confusion, anger and pity. I've wondered if he watched me walk away, with babies in my arms. Did he wish for a different goodbye? Did he call out one last time?

On our last visit, he was at his limit, he was pulling away from life. Dad had come to say goodbye to me, his feisty middle child. My daughters must have been excruciating reminders of the life he'd decided to leave. Looking at a newborn for the first time, especially one you're related to, is a moment of reflection and curious potential. I thought Dad failed to recognize how precious my children were. In retrospect, they were so precious and important to him, he simply couldn't get close. It would have been too painful for him to reach out and witness the promise that lies in the eyes of a child. In all likelihood, it would have only delayed the inevitable.

In truth, he'd lost the will to live years before. Our visit was his last day, last interaction, last chance to find unconditional love and redemption for a life at which he believed he'd failed.

I'll never know if he found peace.

For years I felt guilty about that last visit. I knew he wasn't happy, and I wished I'd been more understanding. I rarely spoke of how he died. I'd lie and say he had a heart attack. It was 10 years before I admitted to anyone that he took his own life. Suicide makes people uncomfortable. It brings up feelings of guilt and fear in others.

On more than one occasion I was asked, "Why didn't you do something to help?" Over time and with life experience, I came to the truth that there's no amount of external love that will fill an internal void. No grandchild, exact words, or perfect visits would have been enough to save him from his inner anguish.

It's heartbreaking that we seem to take the time to discover more about our loved ones only after they've died. After he was gone, I learned about my father's boyhood, what he was like, his interests and hobbies, his friends, and regrettably, the demoralizing treatment he received at the hands of his mother. He was not a loved child. My father was a painful reminder of his brother, who had died of polio. He embodied great loss for my grandmother. He suffered tremendously under her verbal abuse and ran away from home in his early teens.

I was angry at my grandmother for her cruelty toward him. I blamed her for my father's inability to show us love and affection. My father found a way to cope. It came at a cost though. He swallowed the hurt, and it turned toxic. In my father's case, it altered his ability to experience and express love.

In 2010, I traveled to my grandmother's ancestral hometown in Ireland. It was with a stubborn heart I agreed to listen to the story of her childhood from my cousin, the unofficial keeper of our family secrets. Sitting in the dimly lit house where she grew up and hearing about her life's experiences, I became able to forgive my grandmother for her treatment of my father and in turn to forgive my father for leaving us. I came to the realization that my grandmother had been raised in cruelty. Her brother, as the head of the family, treated his sisters with bitterness and contempt. This was a family cycle… Who trained her brother? That I don't know.

There's an old Irish saying: "He left his fiddle at the door." My cousin explained that my grandmother's brother, my great uncle, was the life of the party, laughing and entertaining everyone wherever he went. When he returned to the farmhouse that he shared with his sisters, he symbolically hung his kindness and humour at the door. As a result of his behavior, my grandmother left home when she was a young girl and emigrated to Canada. I see this now as extreme strength. I feel such compassion at the thought of her sorrow over having to leave her family and country. It's not lost on me the bitter irony that my father had to leave home to get away from her.

For me, writing this chapter was both difficult and healing. I didn't want to expose my father to judgment, nor myself to the criticism that can sometimes be directed at family members of those who kill themselves. Writing about our last visit has helped me remember the subtler nuances of who he was as a man—his voice, his limp, his smile.

I believe it is possible to carry wounds in our DNA, which can be passed down from generation to generation. Wounds that have the ability to affect us directly and indirectly. On that final last visit, I was crying out for my father's approval and he desperately wanted mine. Had we known how to communicate and heal our wounds, we could have enjoyed shared communication and deep acceptance of each other and of ourselves.

In understanding my father's and my grandmother's suffering, I found forgiveness and it helped me remember the good in them and their subtle reminders of love.

When I think about my daughter hugging my father for the last time, when I bear witness, countless times, hovering there in that last moment together, I honour his strength and humanity. When I linger in those delicate memories, I feel his pride, his resolute belief in me as a daughter and as a mother. I see with clarity his deliberate love and yes, it was, it is and will continue to be, more than enough.

Scan the QR Code below to view our interview with:

Shauna Marie MacDonald

https://youtu.be/hDVGeLchg2U

Shauna Marie is an author, speaker, mentor and founder of Thrive Beyond Cancer. Shauna Marie teaches the art of embracing the gratitude in adversity in order to live life with ease and purpose.

Shauna Marie finds inspiration in the company of family and friends, writing, experimental cooking and traveling to her beloved Florence, Italy. Shauna Marie walked 800 km through France and Spin on The Camino de Santiago Trail. The pilgrimage was the birthplace of the shift in Shauna Marie's life and career.

Thrive Beyond Cancer, stems from the loss of Shauna Marie's ex-husband from cancer. During the final days of his life, he shared a profound realization that for him "Cancer Gave More Than It Took." Shauna Marie began researching restorative practices to heal Physically Emotionally & Spiritually after a cancer journey: The Eight Pillars to Thrive Beyond Cancer are the result of her findings.

Connect with Shauna Marie

www.shaunamarie.ca

www.facebook.com/shaunamarie8

www.instagram.com/shauna.marie1/

www.linkedin.com/in/shaunamariedesigns/

Chapter 20

#MeToo - How I Healed from Incest to Awaken to the Divine Feminine Within

By Laura J Cornell, PhD

This is my #MeToo story. It's also the story of how I recovered my connection to myself, to my mom, and to the Divine Feminine.

Like all #MeToo stories, this story is not fun to tell. It's gut-wrenching to spell out how bad everything was in my worst moments, as I would prefer to live in the beautiful present, and in gratitude. I am grateful for the present ~ my sweet husband, friends and community that surrounds me, fulfilling work, tender connections with all my family members, a lively connection with my inner life and with Spirit, Source. I have come to be grateful for my past as well, and I realize that my life is blessed.

But I tell this story here as a form of service, for others who may have experienced something similar, and also for myself, as a way of continuing to sew together the pieces of my life.

Experiencing incest broke me apart. Like a frozen river whose deep waters continue to move freely, but whose surface cracks and breaks into jagged chunks, I was unable to deal with the natural flow of my emotions or to face the challenges of adolescence and young adulthood in a healthy way. I turned instead to broken, jagged coping behaviors.

The year is 1978. I am 15 years old and have my first period. I am so embarrassed by my body and its bleeding that I hide my bloody underwear in a drawer. I am so disconnected from my mother that it never occurs to me to tell her, or to ask her to buy me menstrual pads. Somehow, she finds the underwear in the drawer and looks at me in surprise. "Why didn't you tell me?" she asks. I am utterly ashamed.

In my freshman and sophomore years of high school I was lonely, isolated, and afraid to go into the lunchroom. I sometimes eat my lunch hiding in the bathroom. While I do develop close friendships in my junior and senior years, the inner experience of isolation continues.

After high school, I go through several painful years of binge eating, extending into my early 20s. I eat a normal meal, then one dessert, then another, then some more bread, and then another dessert. I hear a distant voice inside my head saying "This is awful. You should stop," but I feel compelled to continue.

Sometimes, I secretly stuff down as many crackers, cookies, chips, and peanut butter as I can find. I am terrified someone will walk in and see me. After one of these episodes, I try to vomit the food up, as I feel sick to my stomach. Fortunately, I'm not able to make myself throw up, or I'm convinced I would have become bulimic.

The final straw is when I come down with pneumonia and then immune fatigue. Just four years after college I get a type of pneumonia that only the elderly or hospitalized usually get. Two rounds of antibiotics later I am still sick. After six weeks, I go back to work as an elementary school teacher, much weakened.

The stress of multiple years of unhealthy eating and little exercise, combined with not having any means to soothe my frayed nervous system, catches up with me. Over the next several years I find myself chronically ill, either having a cold or flu, just getting over one, or about to get one. I see no way out of this state and come to accept it as normal.

My life might have continued this way if not for the grace of an accident at work. I fell and was sent to a chiropractor, who treated not only my back, but diagnosed me with immune fatigue and told me to go to yoga. This was a major turning point that would change the course of my life.

I still remember my first yoga class in 1992. My body was unfamiliar with the poses and many of them felt uncomfortable. But most of all I remember the teacher saying not to compare ourselves with anyone else in the room, but instead to go at our own pace. This self-acceptance was a radical concept for me.

My energy level improved immediately, and I was able to go out dancing the next evening after work, something I hadn't done in years. I quickly became a dedicated yoga practitioner, and a certified instructor 3 years later.

Yoga not only gave me the means to heal my immune and nervous systems, but, helped me to go deeper still. Through yoga I learned to gently access my emotions and explore them within, creating a safe container for integrating painful childhood memories. I would return to this container repeatedly for the next several decades, coming home to myself and over and over again as I untangled the web of my past.

I came to understand what was behind the binge eating, and, was able to release it. I realized that being physically heavy provided some twisted form of safety and security for me. Guys wouldn't notice me, and I didn't have to compete for attention or being liked. I could just be a nobody. As I came to feel safer in my body this became less necessary.

I also realized that by overeating I unconsciously tried to companion my mom, who was constantly going on and off of diets, not happy with her weight. On the one hand, Mom was a beautiful woman who carried herself well. She was a plus-size model for Dillards, participating in fashion shows in exchange for gift certificates. On the other hand, was her repeated dieting.

A therapist helped me see through this. "Don't you think that if you want to companion your mom, she would rather have you happy and healthy?" This was a great insight, and I realized that being my best self ~ not holding myself back ~ was the way to be her friend in life.

As much as yoga was helping me to ground my emotions, I longed for more ways to connect with other women and with my own feminine being. I learned a sequence of yoga poses called the Moon Salutation, which was created to balance and strengthen a woman's body. Fascinatingly, this yoga flow was specifically designed to support the unique phases of a woman's life cycle ~ menstruation, pregnancy, and menopause. For me, doing these poses helped heal the shame and disconnection I had experienced as a teenager about my menstrual flow.

The Moon Salutation was also created to honor feminine values of relationship, openness, and connecting with the earth. The Moon Salutation brings women together in sacred circle, something I dearly love. I decided to write my master's Thesis on this yoga flow, exploring it through interviews with senior yoga teachers as well as through in-depth reading on women's psychology.

As part of this research on women's psychology, I came upon many books on sexual trauma, women's disconnection from our bodies, and incest, all of which I had experienced. While I had discussed the incest in therapy earlier, I came to understand even more clearly how it had affected me, and how important it was to address it directly.

I read that in father-daughter incest, the daughter is cut off from her mother and thus her own inner feminine. This made complete sense to me. I committed to heal my relationship to myself, my mom, and to my own inner Divine Feminine. One step in that healing was telling the truth about the trauma I had experienced as a child.

When I was a toddler my dad had trouble controlling his temper. My sister and I were spanked on multiple occasions, although I have almost no memory of these incidents. I did however, hear my mom repeatedly tell the story of my dad "losing it" on me when I was a toddler. Mom said she had to pull me away from him and that I was black and blue the next day.

For many years she would tell this story as a joke, as if to laugh at what a strange husband she had. Finally, in my late 30s I asked her if that story were true, and she said that yes, it was. I responded, "That's not funny Mom, that's really sad." Mom replied, "I'm sorry. You're right, it's not funny." I never heard her speak of the incident again.

My mom loved her husband dearly, and very much wanted to create a good life with him. But things weren't easy, and raising children is complex. Neither of my parents was well equipped to help my sister and me manage our emotions, love our bodies or learn about sex with grace.

When I was 7 my father decided to "educate" me about the male body, exposing himself to me without telling my mom, and asking if I'd like to touch. Something so out of context with the rest of my life and so unknown to my mom was completely terrifying to me. The only dream I remember from childhood was of my father chasing me with a knife on a burning ship.

When I was a pre-adolescent, it was my dad, not my mom, who talked with me about expecting my period, telling me that he tracked my mom's cycle on his calendar, and that he would be happy to do the same for me. And it was my dad, not my mom, who talked with me about sex and their couple relationship. These conversations humiliated and traumatized me.

My emotions were frozen from these experiences, and I felt existentially lonely from my mom's absence in my life emotionally. Therapy helped me to understand that I needed to tell my mom what had happened. Thankfully, when I told her she believed me, and supported my moving forward in the way that felt right to me.

Discussing the incest wasn't easy for me, and it was several years before I was ready to talk to my dad about it. I first wrote him a letter and awaited his reply. I felt sick to my stomach when I got an envelope in the mail from him, knowing it held his response.

This began a bumpy process of communication. My mom insisted that my dad listen to me and enter into dialogue. We went through a day of family therapy, and at the end he said he understood why his actions were inappropriate. It would be more than a decade later before he was able to express his emotions about all of this, saying he felt "terrible" when he realized he had harmed me.

While things were still bumpy between us for a while, I felt freedom in no longer having a secret to hide. I was grateful to my parents for having extended way beyond their comfort zone to hear me. And I felt empowered in knowing that speaking my truth could have a positive impact on our family.

So many other factors in my life conspired to support me. When I look back, I have a sense of the Divine Mother walking along beside me, pulling me forward toward wholeness.

Despite tremendous inner brokenness, I had a deep desire to connect with others. As a junior in college, I noticed that all of my friends except me were dating, and I decided to do something to change that. I went to the health center and spoke with a therapist, then signed up for a non-credit but comprehensive course on human sexuality. Two months later I found myself head-over-heels in love with a smart, gentle man. We were a perfect match ~ neither of us had ever kissed anyone before ~ and the next two years of puppy love and budding sexuality were incredibly healing.

Other positive factors included my connection with nature, in which I found great peace walking in cornfields, forests, the mountains or by the ocean. My love of movement as a child led to the pleasure I found in dance, which took full bloom later when I learned yoga. Many years of worshiping with Quakers, circling with women, and practicing meditation all helped me come home to the light within, which continues to guide my life to this day.

In 2011 I founded Divine Feminine Yoga to highlight women's healing and empowerment through yoga. To me, Divine Feminine Yoga means embodied wholeness. It's a way of helping ourselves recover from the cultural wound of disconnection from the feminine, the core injury we all experience in patriarchy, no matter the personal details. It's calling ourselves home to befriend our bodies and our inner wisdom. It's locating ourselves as daughters of the Divine

Mother, and as such knowing we are loved and cherished.

I soon became a business coach, supporting other women to strengthen their voice and achieve their purpose in the world. This work has been deeply fulfilling and I love it dearly.

As I grew in my profession, I continued to understand and repair other ways I had been separated from my mom. And as I was growing and wanting to be closer to her, she was growing too. She learned to set boundaries with my dad and to enjoy the company of her children. She loved being a grandma and commented that when she was younger, she had forgotten to enjoy being a mom. I appreciated this insight on her part.

I loved watching the evolution of both of my parents as they grew older. They came to have a beautiful relationship, genuinely enjoying each other's company. They were honest and direct in dealing with conflict, and my dad humble and accepting of my mom's requests, which she was now able to make.

By the time she passed on, my mom and I enjoyed a close relationship. Whereas previously I had rejected her good qualities, I came to admire her deeply, and to want to be more and more like the best of her.

Some of my most tender times with Mom were just after illness or injury, when she would let me care for her gently, just as she must have done for me when I was an infant.

Once when I visited her after a surgery, she joked to the nurses in the hospital that I was going to make her do yoga, and she was right, we did gentle yoga together, right there on her hospital bed. We read her Christian Science Lesson together when I would visit. I just wanted to read whatever my mom was reading, and to accompany her in that.

In her last few years, Mom couldn't reach to touch her feet, and would ask me to put lotion on her dried and cracked toes. I was happy to do this, and to have a way to express my love for her. I soaked her feet in warm salt water, using a brush or pumice stone to remove the dried skin, then would give her a foot massage with olive oil. She loved it.

Through learning to set boundaries and, how to moderate conversations with my dad, I became comfortable with him and for many years now have genuinely enjoyed his company. At the time of my mom's passing, my dad's kindness and spiritual practice were so strong that he was a source of comfort to me and my sister.

I've learned that the gifts of love are not limited to one person. As I learned to love my mom better, I learned to love everyone better, including my dad. Coming home to myself in this way is an ongoing process, day by day and year by year.

The growth and transformation I've had through these experiences are profound. Every day I'm grateful that I can eat a normal meal and then stop. I now honor my body and respect its guidance. I feel an inner peace from my strengthened connection to my mom. I feel the cycles of nature and the Divine Feminine moving through me.

Most importantly, I know my life as sacred.

May all daughters be well supported on their journey, as I have been!

Scan the QR Code below to view our interview with:

Laura Cornell

The Game Changer

https://youtu.be/MEiu4A6O-W4

Laura Cornell, PhD, is an author, speaker, and business mentor who helps women heal ~ body, mind, and soul. She is Founder of Divine Feminine Yoga, where she has directed seven telesummits highlighting women's empowerment through yoga, in addition to leading spiritual immersions and leadership training for women.

In previous work, as Founder of the Green Yoga Association, Laura spurred a national movement towards Green Yoga studios and produced two major conferences on religion and ecology. She has been featured in Yoga Journal, Yogi Times, L.A. Yoga, and Common Ground Magazines.

Laura holds a master's degree in East-West Psychology and a Doctorate in Religion and Philosophy. She is a certified 500-hour yoga teacher and Integrative Yoga Therapist. Her second book, The Moon Salutation: A Woman's Yoga Flow to Heal Herself and Rebalance the World, will be released in 2019.

Laura lives with her husband in Pleasant Hill, California and is inspired by long walks in nature. She has never told her #metoo story before in print.

See Our Other Books in

The Game Changer Series

The Game Changer (Vol. 1) – **https://amzn.to/2q11Vb2**

The Game Changer (Vol. 2) – **https://amzn.to/2CXtQ4b**

Inspired by Iman Aghay

Scan the QR Code below to view our interview with Iman

https://youtu.be/dli72UGR9LA

Made in the USA
Columbia, SC
19 December 2018